CONFESSION AND
THE SERVICE OF
PENANCE

CONFESSION AND THE SERVICE OF PENANCE

F. J. HEGGEN

Translated by Peter Tomlinson

UNIVERSITY OF NOTRE DAME PRESS
NOTRE DAME

First American edition 1968
University of Notre Dame Press, Notre Dame, Indiana

First published 1967
Sheed & Ward Ltd, 33 Maiden Lane, London WC2, and
Sheed & Ward Pty Ltd, 28 Bourke Street, Melbourne

Originally published as *Boete-viering en private biecht*,
J. J. Romen & Zonen, Roermond (1965)

Nihil obstat: Michael Lace, MA, STL, LSS, Censor
Imprimatur: ✠ Patrick Casey, Vic. Gen.
Westminster, 8th February 1967

Library of Congress Catalog Card Number: 67-31394
Printed in the United States of America

Contents

Foreword

This book is the outcome of an encounter between anthropology and theology. Anthropology is the science of man, of the nature of man, which in our time has experienced a significant advance toward greater recognition. Among the consequences of this recognition are genuine difficulties of the faithful regarding the sacrament of penance. One wants to receive this sacrament, but only authentically, not because it has become a habit, not out of an anxious striving for security, but truly as the sign and sacrament of reconciliation with God whenever the relationship with him is interrupted. Although there is widespread rejection of frequent confession, present-day man takes his relationship to God very seriously and wants to put his house in order. That this is so is shown by the search for and the successful exposure of some way to penance outside confession in *Confession and the Service of Penance.*

The evolution of present-day mankind is expressed in the People of God in a development which more and more becomes conscious of itself and thus, we may say, is maturing. For children, therefore, there will be a separation of their first confession and first communion, and the mature Christian will be called to penance in adult responsibility.

Theology itself is cooperating with such a development by preparing the way for a rethinking of the sacraments and their liturgy based on the Vatican Council documents.

This small book by the Dutch Professor Hegen shows the bases, experiences and examples of the pioneering Diocese of Roermond in Holland. The vivid echo to the Dutch forerunners and their widely scattered followers will discover a foundation and an orientation in this book.

Josef Goldbrunner

Preface

In the quest for a living pastoral care and a suitably adapted administering of the sacraments, an important place is claimed by a study of the sacrament of penance. The deadlock which has been reached by traditional confessional practice obliges us to engage upon a basic rethinking and an open dialogue, in which lay Christians have a place. We have in mind the group discussions during the early months of 1963 which were organised by the pastoral advisory committee at Amsterdam—*Gedachten over de prediking van het sacrament van bootvaardigheid,* Hilversum, 1963—as also the pastoral discussions in the diocese of 's-Hertogenbosch, which were concluded by Dr W. Bekkers in his address *Barmhartigheid en biecht* in January 1964. In May 1964, new directives were given for the diocese of Roermond by Mgr P. Moors with regard to children's confession.

This work is intended to be a contribution towards further reflection. It therefore opens with notes on traditional practice, which it considers for the most part obsolete. The second chapter attempts to analyse more closely the basic elements of the conversion to which Christ calls us, and of sin, which he takes upon himself. Finally, from a reflection upon the secularisation of ethics and upon the question which then arises regarding the secularisation of forgiveness, we are led to consider the possibility of a service of penance which is truly contemporary.

These pages find their origin both in lectures given during the academic year 1963–4 to students in theology at Roermond and in a number of addresses to the priests of the diocese.

The theological-pastoral part is followed by several examples of complete services of penance edited by Fr P. J. Mars of Maastricht and myself. A number of the scriptural texts were collected together by theology students at Roermond. We owe our thanks to Fr E. Miedema of Schaesberg for advice on music which may be used during the celebrations.

When we introduced the first Dutch edition of this book we offered it as a contribution towards further discussion. We are aware, as we stated then, that several of the ideas presented here are capable of causing surprise and disagreement. Since then we have sometimes been astonished by what some people have read into our writing, though much more often we have had pleasure in learning of the appreciation and constructive criticism which have come from all sides, often in a most cordial manner. In this connection we are especially grateful to Dr L. Bosse OFM, of Maastricht.

The comments received have persuaded us to give some further explanations and to make a number of additions, which we hope will increase the clarity and consistency of our argument and lessen the danger of misunderstanding. Nowhere have basic alterations been made.

In writing this small book the author has based himself upon his belief in the reality of insufficiency and sin, of grace and new possibilities. It is also in this perspective that he would like it to be understood by priests and others interested in the subject.

Roermond, June 1965

Part 1

Confession
By F. J. Heggen

1
The sacrament
of penance
in tradition

Departure from the traditional practice
of confession

Some time ago Snoeck gave us a short sketch of the
way in which the simple, well-meaning Christian
goes to confession:

> Tomorrow it is Sunday, or monthly communion.
> By midday we say to ourselves that we still have
> to go to confession, or perhaps our wife discreetly
> reminds us. We arrange our work or our errands
> so that the church we like best lies on our way. We
> go in and sit among the row of people waiting be-
> side the confessional of our usual confessor. We
> cross ourselves, consider what we are going to
> say; the same thing, yet again, this and that, so
> many times—not actually done with any real evil
> in mind; we pray a little while, and make an act of
> contrition. When our turn comes we confess our
> sins, hear what our penance is to be, and listen to
> the confessor's few words—with one ear only,
> otherwise we shall forget our penance We say the

act of contrition, glance up a bit relieved, with the happy knowledge that our Lord has granted us pardon and that we are once more at peace with ourselves. We say our penance, stay in the church a little longer to pray, perhaps, for once more we feel that we are standing on the rock of our piety with a clear conscience. Unless we are scrupulous, we now return home in a friendly frame of mind.[1]

This sketch by Snoeck is not yet ten years old; today, however, the confessional practice which he presents as more or less customary appears to us as the traditional one, the old one, once the rule and now the exception. Ten years is a long time in the rapid development which we are experiencing. Anyone reading through the papers and periodicals of 1955 will be astonished when he sees how different the subjects then under discussion were from those of today and how great the distance that we have apparently covered in the intervening period. The custom of monthly confession and communion, to which members of various Catholic organisations were summoned, has been abandoned in most places. More and more Christians are changing over to the integral celebration of mass with communion having been to confession beforehand. But the clearest fact remains that the time is gone when regular devotional confession was accepted more or less without question. At present it is really practised by only a small few. In this respect parishes all show roughly the same picture; the rows of penitents one used to see sitting near the confessionals in almost any church on a Saturday evening, even dur-

[1] A. Snoeck, *Biecht en psychoanalyse*, Bruges (1957), 12.

ing the years after the war, have disappeared. Only a small number still come regularly, and among them are found very few fresh, young people.

Only at the feasts of All Saints, Christmas and Easter do people still go in large numbers to confession. Anyone going into our churches and noting the atmosphere prevailing at these times could easily get the impression that, in fact, during the last twenty years very little has changed in the religious practices of the Catholic population. He probably finds himself in an insufficiently or unevenly lit place, where there are a number of confessionals, each with a number of penitents waiting nearby. He notices nothing on the scene which is suggestive of a liturgical celebration. The penitents present in the church do not form a living community, nor are they united in recognition of their guilt. Many, on entering, glance around quickly; then they go to the place where the smallest number of people are waiting or where the queue is passing through most rapidly. Each one goes through the same ritual, but the visible contact between them is limited to a whispered greeting or a quick nod.

It is a question of how long it will remain the general practice to go privately to confession at least before the great feasts. For it is an unmistakable fact that traditional confessional practice is being subjected to ever-increasing criticism. More and more priests are realising that the experiencing and administering of this sacrament are coming to a deadlock. One does not expect that spite and enmity will come to an end on those days when most people go to confession, but rather when the unsatisfactory elements in our practice are usually strongest felt.

There is already quite a number of truly religious people, authentically 'living the life of the church, who receive this sacrament very seldom, much less often than once a year. They have, as Beemer said in an article published in 1963, the feeling 'that confession does not "fit in with" their religious conviction, that, as it were, the way in which the wood of the confessional box knows sin is different from the way in which they themselves experience their sin; that in the confessional there takes place something to which they remain foreign, whilst, on the other hand, their guilt gets no chance there and finds no escape.'

So that our confessing may be beneficial

Every priest who regularly hears confession will realise, if he seriously reflects on what is, in fact, actual practice, that this sacrament is surrounded by a number of unhealthy situations.

Often confession bears extraordinarily little resemblance to a truly religious event that is carried out in an attitude of prayer and is in positive relation to a fuller and more authentic mode of human existence. Preparation for the reception of this sacrament consists very often in a sort of searching through one's conscience, all too often with a catalogue of sins in hand. But no-one gets to know himself by tracing how often he has *done* this or that, if he does not ask himself what the deed he considers as sinful or as virtuous actually means in his life; why he behaves in such a way, in what direction he is going by acting thus. It is not easy to search one's heart, lay bare one's intentions. But it is without doubt necessary in order for us to see, in some real measure, who we in fact are. It is also a process which sometimes unexpectedly accuses or acquits us. Accuses, where the externally correct deed is unmasked as an affected, clever calculation. Acquits, where the poor result and external failure are recognised as a struggle for goodness and human fellowship. External appearances often deceive; sometimes we are better, sometimes worse, than our behaviour suggests. Going to confession means meeting God as the Father who understands us and accepts us again with love. It is a homecoming; self-evident understanding, care and interest. Christ tells of the sheep which is lost, which is tired and lonely. He searches for it, he carefully carries it to light and warmth. Therefore, when we are preparing ourselves for this sacrament we must not be constantly occupied in reproaching or praising ourselves. When that is the case, it becomes too much of a human achievement, the fulfilling of a duty imposed from without, through all of which it is forgotten that God is the person who acts first.

We must allow ourselves to be found, throw ourselves open to God's coming, for he is going to receive us anew and more lovingly. Confession must be an event in which we pray, considering the care, the goodness, the patience with which God surrounds us in the form of people who show us the face of Christ.

Confession is sometimes hastily and impersonally rushed through. Sometimes due to the penitent, who persists with a stereotyped and noncommittal confession—but who also receives no encouragement to change his approach—or who prefers to come to confession only when matters have become pretty serious. Sometimes it is also the priest who *gets through* as quickly as possible and, on the grounds of tiredness or pressure of work, gives absolution after absolution, without having even made possible a personal contact or a sincere self-expression. The *holy sign* is reduced as far as possible; the priestly prayer for forgiveness and the giving of grace is pronounced in its shortest form and as quickly as possible without the Christian really being able to accept and give assent to it. Thus the impression is often given that frequent confession is of more value than one which is less frequent, but sincerely personal, and in which the proclaiming of mercy by a human person can be experienced as a real message concerning one's concrete existence. Actually it is not strange that many who could not express their shame in words, or whose attempt to do so only gained an incomprehensible formula in reply, do not come any longer. What the second Vatican Council says of the eucharist must also be said of confession:

> The Church, therefore, earnestly desires that Christ's faithful, when present at this mystery of faith, should not be there as strangers or silent spectators. On the contrary, through a proper appreciation of the rites and prayers they should participate knowingly, devoutly, and actively. They should be instructed by God's word. . . .[1]

If we take a look at what people actually confess, we shall perhaps be struck by the unrealistic elements in

[1] *Constitution on the Sacred Liturgy*, II, 48 (as translated in *The Documents of the Vatican II*, ed. Walter M. Abbott, SJ, London and Baltimore (1966), 154).

many confessions, apart from that which is superficial and legalistic about them. This was very rightly pointed out by Brentjens in an article published in 1962: 'the sick confess that they didn't go to church on Sunday, mothers accuse themselves of being distracted in prayer, the soldier says that he swore whilst in fact he used strong language on account of his impatience. A young lad confuses impure thoughts with a healthy appreciation of sex, and the father of a large family can be expected to get annoyed with his children at least once.' Here, in fact, it is neither sin nor unwillingness, nor hardly even insufficiency that is being confessed, but completely normal, healthy, human reactions. Is there a real mother who does not continually carry her concern for her family with her, wherever she goes; and where is the normal father who lets anything and everything pass? Without doubt, there do exist mothers who are too anxious and fathers who are too irritable; in such cases insufficiency and perhaps unwillingness are present.

Do we sufficiently realise what we are actually doing when we ask or pronounce forgiveness for these completely normal facts, which we cannot regret, which in all probability we cannot do without in our lives? A sacrament may not be administered 'just as a matter of course' with the attitude that even if it is not doing much good, it is not doing any harm. Since it is precisely a holy sign, it may only be given in an exceptional situation and where human dignity is assured. When someone goes and confesses intrinsically healthy reactions as sin, not only does a (further) deformation of conscience take place, but also Christianity is experienced as anti-

human; when that which is healthy and spontaneous is expressed and accepted as censurable, then
it is unavoidably suggested that being a Christian
must alienate man from himself.

Confessions often remain stiffly conventional,
whilst in sermons from the pulpit or personal con-
versations no invitation is made to a deepening of
awareness. There are whole fields which are hardly
ever touched: the conscientious carrying out of one's
occupation, honesty in business matters, respect and
co-operation among those who live under the same
roof, mutual understanding between different generations, the authenticity of religious experience.
Mainly more or less stereotyped, external facts are
confessed, whilst the meaning in this life of an
ambiguous happening is not sought after in a reflection which touches a person's heart and the
background to his deeds.

We certainly agree with the opinion that the priest
must take the penitent's honesty seriously. 'Enquir-
ing' and certainly 'cross-examining' are out of place.
But this is not to say that he must simply accept as
authentic the confession presented. The priest
should be aiding the penitent in the formation of his
conscience. This implies that he must try to free him
from an actualistic conception of sin, that he will
take a close look at the confession more often, so
that all that the person in question can feel no
sorrow for may be kept out of the confessional.
He will also draw his attention more often to his
responsibility with regard to other or broader fields
of human existence.

We must realise that a permissive attitude towards legalistic and magic practices only furthers a

discrediting of confession, just when it is being realised that it could be of value at the important moments of life. The person who arrives at a recognition of the unrealistic character of many practices which in general are all too readily accepted, will often also no longer go to confession once he has discovered the guilt of his life and is now searching for salvation.

The diversity of expectations of those who confess frequently

There are doubtless many Christians who even to-day attribute an important place in their lives to regular confession, not because of an impersonal loyalty to an old custom, nor as the exercise of a piety which can hardly be said to have anything of a contemporary character. Presently we shall have an opportunity of reflecting on some of the circumstances which have contributed to making frequent devotional confession a more or less general phenomenon. Now, however, we wish to focus attention on the fact that the real reasons which people have in desiring private confession can be of widely divergent nature.

First of all, it is certainly possible that confession may play a real part in the struggle a person has in attempting to make his or her life more and more into a personal following of Jesus Christ. What Paul writes to the Christians at Rome is true for all of us: 'We were buried therefore with him by baptism into death, so that as Christ was raised from the dead by the glory of the Father, we too might walk in newness of life' (Rom 6: 4). This demands a constant effort. One has to be ready to 'work at oneself' sincerely and with a certain tenacity, so that one's disposition, one's attitude and consequently also one's outward behaviour may increasingly be decided by love, by real devotion and openness to one's fellow human beings. The person who goes to confession in the course of this struggle may perhaps in the first place be seeking personal contact, the testing of his judgement of conscience and encouragement in the hard fight to make authentic respect for his fellow men the central intention of his life. He will look forward to the formal, God-given proclamation of mercy, encouragement and salvation for his life.

A frequent confession can be authentic and healthy for many. But we cannot determine abstractly how often will be best for them, as Canon Law still presumes to do for priests and religious. It is quite obvious that the optimum can differ noticeably from person to person and certainly pronouncing a specific number is in this case not a very helpful thing to do. The definition of an optimum frequency for this or that particular man or woman will have to be made in direct relation to their ability to really engage themselves and keep up their intention. What is good for one can for the very next person be paralysing. Personally, I am under the impression that a particular 'chunk of life', a certain new experience, another living situation or at least an event that grasps us in some real way is desirable in order for confession to be beneficial and inspiring.

It is possible that someone may have come to a real knowledge of personal guilt: that through some incident or another, through a decision that he has taken, through meeting another person, he has received the gift of the Holy Spirit and sees clearly the meaning of his life. Having come to repent, he wishes to rid himself of his guilt by confessing it to another person whom he sees as a man of God and from whom he expects words of salvation and forgiveness.

Here a confession will really be in place, precisely because it is the most obvious, most expressive way in which reconciliation can be asked for by the person who has become conscious of having failed in his personal deeds as a member of the community; for these deeds were the expression of a disposition which goes against the community. When we know ourselves to be seriously guilty it is our duty to come forward and ask to be allowed to live once more in unity with others.

Moreover, some people have need of the self-expression of confession because of the psychological situation they are in. There are many who are lonely and find no-one in their immediate circle who will quietly listen to them with interest. It is only normal that a person should like to chat and unburden himself. Some desires and difficulties, which are in point of fact perhaps not very great ones, they just cannot get off their chest, even to their husband or wife, or closest friend. With these they seek the silence and semi-darkness of the confessional. The person most likely to do this is the one who is carrying with him through life the memory of something about which he is ashamed, that depresses him or causes a nervous uneasiness within him. In this case it is above all a question of 'expressing' it, of 'getting something off one's chest' in a great desire for contact and frankness between oneself and an understanding fellow human being.

In the novel *The Shoes of the Fisherman* by Morris West, Kiril I makes a note in his diary on the evening of his coronation as pope: 'I must ask Rinald to find me a wise priest to whom I can confess myself each day, not only for absolution and the sacramental grace, but for a purging of this pent, stopped-up spirit of mine.'[1] Many are moved by the same considerations to seek confession. They seek wisdom, enlightenment, advice on the difficult questions of life, perhaps, at least at the moment when they are a little obsessed with themselves or with the weight of responsibility that may be pressing on them all too heavily. They want to 'express themselves', they expect encouragement and support for their task, so that they can once more consider it as their calling and their mission.

The priest in the confessional often has to listen to self-accusations which he finds he can only judge as inauthentic and of neurotic origin. Here it may be observed that the confessional situation is not suitable for helping people with disturbed minds and that in actual fact here the need which exists is not for forgiveness of sins but for treatment of illness.[2] It remains equally true that in many cases it is to the priest that a need is first clearly revealed. In this event it is clearly his task to accept the sick person and accompany him in his search for help, which in practice often means inducing the person to place himself under expert treatment.

[1] M. West, *The Shoes of the Fisherman*, London (1963), 78.
[2] See Snoeck, 65.

The confessional situation requires a personal pastoral care

It may seem as if we have strayed off course in considering more closely the real meaning that regular confession can have for some people: the lonely seek contact, those who live under pressure ask for help, the inwardly disturbed desire catharsis, the sick hope for a cure, those who are devout need the company of encouragement, and the person who is aware of his guilt seeks forgiveness. Now it is not our intention to insinuate that the desires listed above as being sought after in confession do not in actual fact have anything in common with each other. A nucleus of real awareness of guilt can also be at play, to a greater or less extent, in those who seek contact, help or cure.

I find it noticeable that during the last few years it has very often been stated that even private confession must first and foremost be a religious event. 'Confession is not a matter of washing, neither is it a complete stock-taking, nor a nice chat, nor a spiritual tête-à-tête. Nor in the first place spiritual guidance. Such uses devalue this sacrament. Faith in the real bringing about of salvation by this particular sacrament must make the practice of confession into an earnest prayer. What a man must do is to throw himself open to God's wonders. The priest's role in this sacrament is that of an intermediary.'[1] I readily agree with the substance of this statement; the actual con-

[1] De Pastorale Adviesraad to Amsterdam, *Gedachten over de prediking van het sacrament van boetvaardigheid*, Hilversum (1963), 19. See also W. Bekkers, *Barmhartigheid en biecht*, St Michielsgestel (1963), 12.

fession must not resemble a cataloguing of one's deeds as good or bad. As if it were possible! A person must put his heart to the test, carefully gauge his attitude in order to see to some extent how far his falling short of the mark in fact meant a renunciation of his intention to love. The dialogue between penitent and priest must not be of a lax and aimless nature: here two people have a task to engage in so that together in openness towards God they may be able to obtain a clear view of their actual mission in life. The forgiveness which is proclaimed to the community in the name of Jesus Christ must form, for human experience also, the culminating point of the whole event.

Having established this, we should like to emphasise that in confession there is need for the exercise of an authentic pastoral care. A short while ago this was clearly indicated from the Protestant side by Roscam Abbing:

> The care given by the church to someone who comes to confess his sins must be deep and comprehensive and must not, therefore, merely contain the giving of absolution, but must also include an intense pastoral concern. A confessional procedure in which the penitent only names his sins and the most the confessor does is to ask questions in order to get other sins confessed and to gauge the penance, so as to then give absolution, strikes us, if only from the pastoral point of view, as unjustifiable. It is precisely those wishing to confess who are often most in need of pastoral care.[1]

[1] P. Roscam Abbing, *Biecht en absolutie*, The Hague (1958), 12–13. In considering this point we have relied on this author amongst others.

The priest must at least to some degree realise the real reason for which a person comes to confession. He should try to sense something of the role which this particular Christian by now expects him to play —not as though he ought purely and simply to fulfil that role, but so as to relate himself to it and use it as starting-point for further guidance. Doubtless, this implies that the administration of confession must take place without haste. The concentration of so many confessions on only a few days of the year— just before All Saints, Christmas and Easter—is highly undesirable because it cannot but further an impersonal and magical experiencing of the sacrament. It is precisely on these days, when so many come to confess, that carefully arranged services of penance can be held, in which no opportunity will usually be offered for individual confession, the emphasis being laid instead upon joint reflection by all the faithful and upon the general confession of guilt and proclamation of grace.

When the priest limits himself, in the administering of penance, to a more-or-less general exhortation and the giving of absolution, during which time the penitent makes an act of contrition—which is, after all, usually the case—then the sign of forgiveness becomes too mechanical and a personal assent is hardly possible. It cannot be said that there has been a proclamation of salvation which can really be lived and experienced when the only answer to what is perhaps a laborious expression of loneliness, failure, poverty and guilt is a formula, which may be very meaningful in itself, but which to the person in question is cold and anonymous. The priest's task here is to be intermediary, and it is precisely for this reason that he will feel bound to exercise truly pastoral care. In his attitude, in the concern he shows towards this person it is the love and generosity of God himself that must find expression. We call Jesus Christ *Emmanuel, God-with-us*. As Anderson remarked in an article in 1963, in Christ's love, in his intense concern for people 'God's love appeared amongst us in visible form, so that in him the earth is filled with God's mercy. Thus the love of Christ is in the fullest sense the sacrament of God's saving love, realising saving love in human form.'

That which held good for the life of Jesus in his relations with others, must also hold good for his church. She is related to him; called as the bearer and witness of the good news to work for truth and freedom in the world; in duty bound to give expression to God's love for us, to make it into historical reality capable of being experienced. It is only when she does this that she is true to her Lord, in whom the goodness and loving kindness of God the Father appeared (Tit 3:4). Only then does she continue his work and bring salvation to human beings. When she administers a sacrament, a sign of God's goodness and Christ's presence, she must in the administering itself make it a living, expressive *revelation* of concern and charity. In the words of Schillebeeckx:

The essential reality . . . is outwardly expressed in the reception of each of the sacraments is . . . the entry into living contact with the visible Church as the earthly mystery of Christ in heaven. To receive the sacraments of the Church in faith is therefore the same thing as to encounter Christ himself.[1]

This may be fact, but it is also and equally injunction and task. The priest must not be satisfied with pronouncing a formula. He will have to be aware that ordination and appointment alone are not yet enough to make him capable of granting forgiveness in the name of God. This he will have to learn time and time again in the realisation of his own sinfulness and of God's infinite kindness. In his attitude, his devotion to humanity, he must give this prayer shape so that forgiveness can be experienced. Then he is imitating Christ. His words of forgiveness were an expression of his whole person, which went out to the sinner. In him God's mercy was made really transparent, so that whoever received pardon from him went home really consoled.

The universal human need of salvation as the starting-point for a further reflection

We wish now to proceed further and penetrate deeper into the actual problem of penance. Above, we have drawn attention to the deadlock often reached in the experiencing and ministration of confession. We have indicated the variety of motives which can be present in a desire for confession and have here added a plea for pastoral care in the administering of this sacrament. It is now our intention to raise for discussion a few questions concerning the place which confession can take in the life of adult Christians today and the form in which

[1] E. Schillebeeckx, OP, *Christ the Sacrament*, London (1963), 64.

it can be experienced.[1] We are interested not in the restoration of an old usage, but in a consideration of the question: How can this sacrament be a real means of grace and at the same time bring salvation which is capable of human experience? There is need of salvation today, just as much as before.

Every normal human being finds that he is called to live in the company of others. He knows the good that can be done by the charity and understanding which people show towards him. He remembers the joy and peace received at some time through opening his heart and truly making another person his neighbour. But he also knows that he is continually falling short: however good his intentions may be, he nevertheless causes others pain. He does not give them what they actually need. Sometimes it is only with great difficulty that he manages to stand by those who are nearest and dearest to him. Every parent knows that there are days on which he clearly experiences an inability to give positive support to his child. Everyone who really likes another person knows just how short the periods of real openness towards one another are and how much, even then, one continues to go one's own way, regardless of others.

We are a support for each other, but also a burden. We cause one another pain, not just in ways which we could have avoided, which thus bring guilt upon ourselves, but also in ways which are inevitable. No-one can go through life without getting his hands dirty, nor without knowing loneliness and

[1] For a discussion concerning children's confession we refer to our contribution *Intocht der kinderen*, Roermond (1964).

enmity. This means that in point of fact none of us can live without longing for grace, charity and forgiveness for the disruption of our existence; a disruption which we carry with us as our inescapable lot, which we try to overcome by really living for others, by being good, friendly and true, but a disruption which we also confirm by making ourselves the centre of all existence and by using others for our own purpose.

The way in which the sacrament of penance was experienced in earlier generations: continuity and change

The history of ecclesial administering of forgiveness is both long and full of variation. It is hardly important to note that the confessional, which not a single church lacks today, is of quite recent origin. In fact, it first appeared in the sixteenth century and only through the insistence of the Council of Trent and the publication of the *Rituale Romanum* was it gradually introduced everywhere.

More important is the fact that so-called devotional confession—the frequent sacramental confession of venial sins—first came into fashion rather late. It was not known to the early church. The apostolic and post-apostolic writings make only a few, widely scattered remarks on the nature and place of penance, so that we cannot form a really clear picture of the actual form it took. What may be said with certainty, in our opinion, is that already in the New Testament writings we can discover some basic indications: every sin requires a penance, but no sin is really unforgivable (Jas 1: 21; 5: 19; 2 Pet 3: 9; 1 Jn 2: 1ff.)—prayer, works of mercy and the intercession of the community of the faithful obtain forgiveness of sins (1 Jn 5: 14ff.; Jas 5: 14ff.); in the case of serious sins, certainly in the case of sins which give scandal, it is the duty of the leader of the community to reprimand, and eventually to resort to exclusion from the company of the *saints* (1 Cor 5: 3ff.; 2 Cor 2: 5-11; 12: 21; Jas 1: 21; 5: 19; 2 Pet 3: 9).

From the third century there have been preserved numerous witnesses concerning ecclesial penance. Nevertheless, even today there still exists no real consensus on how these sources should be interpreted and estimated in comparison with each other. In various periodicals discussion still continues, for example, on the question of whether all sins could be forgiven by ecclesial penance, which sins were of necessity subject to this penance; how the confession took place—whether before the official minister alone, or in certain areas and for certain sins, also before the whole community.

It was mainly from the fourth century on that the practice of ecclesial penance became subject to more and more precise rules, which were increasingly generalised. It was universal practice that a person might only once in his life be admitted to ecclesial penance. A repetition was thought undesirable, sometimes on the grounds of Augustine's opinion that a means of cure which is often used loses its power, sometimes following the theory of Ambrose and many others, namely that the penitent is permanently stamped by the 'second baptism'—as a certain sort of Christian with less rights. It is 'the second stage of salvation after the shipwreck of sin'. Moreover, children's confession was something completely unknown. Some church gatherings expressly recommended that young people should never be admitted to ecclesial penance, even when they had been guilty of grave offences and had become seriously ill. For in any case, even after reconciliation and readmittance into the church the former penitent remained under very heavy obligations which cut him off from the world. Many occupations were closed to him and he was permanently forbidden marital relations. Priests and candidates for the priesthood, to whom the present ecclesiastical laws strongly recommend frequent confession, were forbidden public penance by the early church.

In the early Middle Ages the Anglo-Saxon monks spread another form of penance over the mainland of western Europe. This new practice differed from the old in that it could be used more often and by all the faithful, even including the clergy, in that the status of public penitent and its lasting obligations no longer existed, and finally, the intervention of a priest was sufficient on its own. One's sins were confessed to the priest, who also represented the community of the faithful, and directly after the confession of sins he would announce forgiveness and reconciliation, without waiting for the penance imposed to be fulfilled.[1]

[1] We cannot give here a detailed survey of the history of ecclesial penance. We refer those interested in the subject to: Paul Anciaux, *The Sacrament of Penance*, Challoner Publications, Tenbury Wells (1962); John Kelly, *Early Christian Doctrines*, Adam and Charles Black, London (1958); B. Poschmann, *Poenitentia Secunda*, Bonn (1940); and *Penance and the Anointing of the Sick*, Burns and Oates, London (1964); C. Vogel, *Le Péché et la Pénitence*, Tournai (1961), 147–235.

Through the centuries one sees an unmistakable shift in the estimation of what constitutes the actual substance of the sacrament. During the first stage of the existence of aural confession the emphasis clearly lay upon atonement. Achievement of the penance was seen as the actual forgiving element. In the *Libri Poenitentiales* especially, the idea is often given that a person can be more inwardly sure of the forgiveness of his sins and readmittance into the community of the church in the measure that he has performed heavier penances.[1] In a second period it is more the confession that appears as the forgiving element. This becomes the greatest penance that someone can achieve, consisting of shame and humiliation, which are made more profound in the measure that one goes into more personal detail. It seems highly probable that it was during this time— in the eleventh and twelfth centuries—that the confession of 'venial sins' was widely encouraged. In the early church and that of the early Middle Ages the ecclesial confessing of mortal sins, or at least of certain very serious offences, was considered necessary, and it was taught that lesser transgressions could be forgiven through private penitential practices, such as almsgiving, fasting and prayer. Only when the confession became in the first place a penance did a sort of devotional confession come

[1] This can be studied more closely in H. Schmitz, *Die Bussbücher und die Bussdisciplin in der Kirche*, Graz (1961). This work certainly offers the most complete survey of the ancient *Libri Poenitentiales*; it dates from 1883, however, and is not always sufficiently critical. A very recent work which in our opinion is most trustworthy is L. Bieler, *The Irish Penitentials*, Dublin (1963). One can also find considerable information in the works of Poschmann mentioned above.

into fashion. Often this was not made before a priest, but before a person not holding an office, a layman. The confession came first and the qualities of the person to whom the confession was made were held to be of rather minor importance, although the actual power to absolve continued to be reserved to bishop and priest.

In the third period, repentance was considered the most important element; God gives heed first and foremost to the heart of a person, to his intention. This latter induces him humbly and sincerely to confess to the priest the guilt of which he is conscious and to accomplish faithfully the penance imposed.

During the centuries in which a decisive importance was attributed to repentance, the nature of this repentance was also questioned—how deep it must penetrate into someone's heart in order for him to be granted God's forgiveness. But the church lived through twelve or thirteen centuries without the clear awareness of this distinction, which appeared so important to later generations that they drew it to the attention of their children whilst these were yet infants.

Change which preserves what is good, so that this good may be constantly made present

All these changes in external form and inward estimation make it clear that the sacrament of penance is something living, which stands in a history that is continually changing and constantly renewing itself. The Council of Trent laid down that the sacraments of the New Testament were all instituted by Christ and that in consequence the church does not possess power to change the actual substance of the sacraments.[1] But history clearly shows us that we must not think that the sacraments were determined by the Lord in their present-day, sharply differentiated forms. Christ lives in his church; it is her gift and at the same time her task to render the love of God, which appeared unsurpassably in Jesus, present to the world. God has need of human beings. 'God's operation of salvation needs man's co-operation. For God is no magic power, but a mystery of word and love . . . God's saving presence in the world takes place through the mediation of real, historically situated human beings; in the Old Testament through Israel with its men of God . . .; when the fullness of time came, through Jesus Christ, the Word who became man; and after the resurrection of the Lord, through the church, God's new Israel.'[2] This church is founded on Christ, she is the community of those who are called together by his spirit into one body and one love. For whatever she has she owes thanks to him. That which lives in her is the gift of his Spirit. Therefore, in the celebration of the sacraments, in which her express wish is to grasp, bless and raise men's lives to Christ's loving zeal, she knows herself to be dependent in an extraordinary way upon her Lord. But 'the church, taken as "a spiritual house, built of living stones"—1 Pet. 2: 5—is never finished. From generation to generation, true to

[1] Denzinger-Schönmetzer, 844.
[2] A. Dondeyne, 'De praktische verhouding tussen ambtsdrager en leek', *Tijdschift voor Theologie*, 2 (1962), 248.

tradition, she is continually being made anew; just as the human race is never complete, but is constantly reviewing the nature of human existence and living in accordance with its new insight'.[1] As something which enters and participates in the history of man, the church is subject to a continual process of change and renewal. She must be subject to it in order that she may be a faithful bride to the Lord and a visible sign of God's presence among men. What is true of the church must also be true of her sacraments. The varying history of penance convinces us of the fact that it can, or rather must, have a new future, just in the same way as it has had an ancient and sometimes unrecognisable past.

The alterations which this sacrament has undergone in the course of history have been so fundamental and far-reaching that many theologians would have held them impossible—seeing their ideas on the immutable substance of the sacraments —if they had not been compelled by the facts to accept them as so-called accidental alterations. We cannot here and now establish, *a priori*, on the basis of our present knowledge, the changes in form which are or are not possible for the future. Neither can history offer us any definite answer to this question. Whether the early or medieval church knew liturgical services of penance, with or without private confession, is therefore not of decisive importance. As Fr Van den Baar commented in an article in 1965, we should ourselves be guilty of a foolish historicism and give evidence of a fundamental misunderstanding of the historicity of truth in the church, were we to go searching for concrete

[1] A. Dondeyne, 250.

answers to our present-day, concrete questions in a tradition which has not been confronted with this sort of problem and whose religious sensibility often differs from ours in a most clear-cut way. If we believe in the presence of the Spirit of Christ in his church, then we must know that we cannot predetermine or foretell the activity of that Spirit. It is he who gives us room in which to feel our way towards new forms, in which salvation and forgiving love can become reality for the present generation.

Circumstances which have promoted frequent devotional confession

We need only go one step back in history to find ourselves in a time when frequent private confession was accepted and practised more or less without any problem. But although the distance between that period and the one in which we live is not great when measured in years, there is a clear difference in atmosphere and climate. Without intending to present an exhaustive investigation, we now wish to indicate several factors which a short while ago formed current elements of Catholic preaching and experience and which worked in favour of frequent devotional confession. Through this we hope to contribute towards a balanced estimation of the deadlock which in reality exists concerning confession.

The 'power' of the sacrament and man's personal effort. Nowadays, theologians in general refuse to accept any conception which sees the sacrament of penance primarily as an external means of salvation, as a sort of means of replacement for personal repentance. In theory everyone knows that not even the priest's absolution can forgive sin which a person has not inwardly moved away from by real contrition. In fact, the impression is equally often given that the sacrament offers the possibility of getting by, 'as an easier path to salvation, a sort of system by which we can get grace more abundantly for less loyalty in God's service'.[1] It is said, in the words of the Council of Trent, that the sacrament gives grace 'to those who present no obstacles'. Schillebeeckx is of course right in remarking that this negative expression—one might almost wish to say 'passive approach'—should be understood positively: 'not to hinder grace means, for an adult, a positive personal intent'.[2] The terminology usually employed has often in fact suggested to many Christians that the sacrament must contain something of an automatic effect. In the Dutch Catechism of 1948 children are told: 'For a good confession imperfect contrition is enough. Through perfect contrition we receive forgiveness of mortal sins, even outside confession.'[3] Doubtless, in the further elaboration of this teaching, it is possible to explain theoretically that this sacrament can in no sense be a means of replacing personal repentance. When one consults the theological treatises on this point, however, one quickly finds oneself in a theological atmosphere which is so rarefied that many people cannot breathe in it. In general it is insufficiently made clear how—from the psycho-

[1] E. Schillebeeckx, *Christ the Sacrament*, 166.
[2] Schillebeeckx, 166.
[3] See the answers to questions 308 and 309, as also the answers to questions 293 and 294 in the CTS catechism.

logical point of view, that is—an imperfect contrition can, through and in the sacrament, grow to the depth of a perfect contrition: 'The effect of the sacrament of confession is the infusion of sanctifying grace and the cancelling-out of sins *thereby*; now, the infusion of sanctifying grace converts imperfect contrition into perfect contrition . . . thus the effect of the sacrament of confession is that imperfect contrition is converted into perfect contrition and that *thereby* sins are forgiven.'[1]

Would it not be better to abandon discussions and explanations concerning perfect and imperfect contrition? The emphasis should be laid upon the necessity for sincere repentance. This means a repentance which is not egocentric in character. It is quite normal that a person's repentance should only come about hesitatingly and should slowly penetrate deeper. From a regret which is predominantly concern for oneself, one grows to the realisation that one has neglected or failed to appreciate one's task in the human community. As long as this self-concern predominates and the actual centre of the guilt is not attacked there is no resumption or deepening of one's fundamental option in life and no re-establishment in love can take place. No-one can be forced into love and human fellowship. What is possible is that, through the openness and charity with which another—and thus ultimately God—addresses us, a development within our heart may be set in motion or speeded up, or made more intense. Forgiveness is possible ultimately because our

[1] P. Schoonenberg, 'Het volmaakt en onvolmaakt berouw', *Jaarboek Werkgenootschap katholieke theologen in Nederland*, Hilversum (1952), 132.

neighbour, our God, believes in us, more firmly entrusts us with a task in church and world, and because we give our glad assent.

Significance of confession for the forgiving of sins; the priest's function with regard to the penitent. In addition to traditional theory, and especially traditional understanding, about perfect and imperfect contrition, and the power attributed to them of obtaining forgiveness *within* and *outside* the sacrament, the frequent practice of the sacrament was also stimulated by a particular appreciation of actual confession and of the priestly function in connection with it.

We have already indicated that in the Middle Ages one encounters the opinion that the forgiveness of sins becomes more complete and more general in the measure that shame increases; which can be achieved by confessing one's sins to as many people as possible as often as possible and as accurately as possible. In an altogether moderate work, *The Instruction of Youth in Christian Piety*, which first appeared in France in 1665, it is stated concerning confession and its completeness:

It will serve to give him [the confessor] a perfect knowledge of your conscience, that he may better direct you, and give you advice according to your necessity. . . . With regard to God; it will be a means of meriting from him more to bring about for your more perfect conversion. These graces he will communicate to you in proportion as he shall see you humbled before him. . . .[1]

[1] Charles Gobinet, *The Instruction of Youth in Christian Piety*, Dublin (1793), 51.

Here the actual confession itself is the means *par excellence* of obtaining the forgiveness of sin.

Thus it is considered normal procedure that the priest should ask very concrete questions. He is called, in his juridical function, to pass judgement, it is said, and must therefore be in a position to pass judgement. Even in this day and age, a widely distributed and much reprinted German book can say:

> Confession is a judgement (*Buszgericht*), God's judgement, and at the same time a self-judgement on myself: the judge is Christ himself, the priest is only his representative, his instrument. I am the accused and at the same time my own accuser.[1]

For centuries confession was an instrument of guidance in the first place and in undesirable cases an instrument of control. Here a person could be protected against the influence of the Reformation, here he could be sheltered from the effect of undesirable contacts. Now this practice must without doubt be judged in the perspectives of the period in which it arose and was accepted. Earlier society was more primitive than ours; the priest was then socially more qualified to lead than he is today; people lived in a less democratic structure and had perhaps more need for concrete directives than later generations. The great manuals of moral theology also generally insisted upon moderation and discretion in the interrogation of the penitent.

Nevertheless, it is not to be wondered at that in our society this confessional practice is being

[1] G. Hopfenbeck, *Männerbeichte*, Augsburg (1963⁹), 47.

accepted only with ever-increasing difficulty. It made the priest into a judge and the penitent into a humbled person who, in fear of a severe judgement, had to reveal great pieces of his intimate life to the priest. This is something which modern man will more and more resist.

A predominantly actualistic and one-sidedly super-naturalist experience of sin. A third series of factors favouring frequent confession relates to the notion and experience of sin. Discussion on the secularisation of the awareness of sin and the varying degrees of personal guilt—both, in our opinion, very important for the 'estimation' of confession—we reserve for the following chapters.

Often it is quite plainly and precisely stated that frequent confession is necessary simply in order to live a justifiable life. Thus we read in *The Instruction of Youth in Christian Piety*:

Because although you may be some time without falling into mortal sin, nevertheless without frequent confession you may fall into a great number of venial sins, which being multiplied and neglected lead to mortal sin. Without frequent confession you may be secretly engaged in wicked habits, which you will not believe to be such, and will be exposed to many dangerous occasions, against which you cannot guard yourself unless you be admonished. Now you cannot be admonished, but by often discovering your conscience to a discreet confessor, who will observe them, and warn you to avoid them. It is impossible that you should continue long without being assaulted by temptations, and particularly against chastity.

Now it is impossible you should resist them without frequent confession. Do what you will, if you make not often use of this remedy you will infallibly fall, as experience will convince you.[1]

We believe that this quotation may be considered as typical of a long period. The indispensable requirement of concrete guidance by a priest which we have indicated above is brought out clearly by it.

Past centuries laid strong emphasis upon the purity of conscience which was required for the reception of the eucharist. Doubtless, Catholic tradition rejected the Jansenist conception whereby the eucharist, being 'the bread of angels', might only be partaken of by those who had arrived at a definitive victory over their 'sinful passions' and had reached a real degree of perfection. And yet several centuries in the history of the church show rigoristic traits in this matter. For a good many generations it was the custom, at least for Christians in the world, that one did not go to communion unless one had been to confession the evening before. It was pretty generally accepted that one moment in a person's life could decide their eternal destiny. How many people, even now, ask the priest fearfully whether doing this or doing that is a mortal sin? Life still continues to be seen by many, as Anderson said, 'as a series of detached deeds, some of which are mortal sins, that will be presented to us later like an account. On this account hell is seen as a punishment for separate mortal sins. It is forgotten that sin cannot be viewed separately from the person and his basic disposition.' How fearfully many stood

[1] Gobinet, 53.

before the God of love can be felt to some degree when we hear old people who have been brought up in fear. God's wrath has often been more loudly proclaimed than his love and benevolent presence.

Especially in the practice of moral education a heavy accent has often been laid upon the will of God as a source of, and foundation for, good and evil. Thus we used to say: 'Lying is a sin and God doesn't allow that.' This brings about the effect that a person easily considers himself guilty directly and almost exclusively before God and is then apt to seek forgiveness by going directly, in confession, to him and his representative; not to mention the inherent inaccuracy of such a view, which concerns itself too little about providing a real insight into the reason behind the moral obligation. The faithful were also advised to say in the evening an act of contrition once more and to join in a recitation of the *Confiteor* of the mass, but too little attention was given to the fact that lying means being evil to another person and that turning back from a lie demands a turning back to that other person. Where was forgiveness granted to the man who had insulted his wife? Was this experienced in the embrace of two people who had rediscovered each other, or did one think that one ought to experience it in the formula of absolution spoken by the priest?

2
Basic elements of human sinfulness and conversion

Jesus' call to conversion concerns all of us

According to the witness of the gospels, John the Baptist preached a baptism of conversion for the forgiveness of sins. Mark tells us of Jesus' first appearance in Galilee: 'And he said, "The time is fulfilled, and the kingdom of God is at hand; repent, and believe in the gospel" ' (Mk 1: 15). Peter concludes his address at Pentecost to the inhabitants of Jerusalem with the appeal: 'Repent, and be baptized every one of you in the name of Jesus Christ for the forgiveness of your sins' (Acts 2: 38).

When one reads scripture, one hears the call to conversion to change one's life to follow Jesus. No exceptions are made. We have all to strive towards a change of mentality. All self-satisfaction is denounced. The story of the pharisee and the tax collector is introduced by the observation: 'He also told this parable to some who trusted in themselves that they were righteous and despised others' (Lk 18: 9). The old Jewish plan of salvation is broken through in the New Testament. It is the breaking through of a juridical and quantitative conception of sin, which leaves a person under the impression that he is fundamentally righteous and yet at the same time shows only typical weaker points. In all that we do, limitation and sinfulness cling to us. According to the scribes, one could divide people into two groups; namely, the righteous, who make themselves righteous by faithfulness to the law, and the sinners, who go against the law. In the preaching of John and of Jesus the call to conversion is directed towards all men, towards each of us.[1]

We must be ready to be influenced by what scripture proclaims and to accept it as a correction to our spontaneous tendency towards self-excuse. During the last decades we have gained a sharper insight into the complexity of human behaviour and motivation. We are beginning to discover how much fear, involuntary reaction and inward disturbance there can be behind outwardly destructive action and negative behaviour. We have obtained a readier perception of the inextricable solidarity of collective and personal responsibility, now we are realising 'that society as a whole, thus all of us without exception, are to a great extent—if not personally, then at least collectively, co-responsible for all injustice, crime and wrongdoing occurring amongst us'.[2]

Every human being who takes a critical look at his own existence knows that he falls below the mark. He causes pain to others or leaves them in loneliness.

[1] See especially Mt 3: 1–12; Mk 1: 2–8; Lk 3: 1–18 for this universal call to conversion.
[2] C. Trimbos, *Misdaad zonder straf?*, Utrecht (1962), 6.

He is often powerless, not able to meet another's need. He knows that when he goes in one direction to help someone, in another direction there is some-one else who is dear to him and rightly longs for his support, whom he must abandon. Experiences like these, which really do happen, sometimes tempt us into losing sight of the reality of guilt, of shortcomings to which we give assent. The message of scripture counters this temptation.

> Christianity reveals this. Man is above all a being who chooses, even in the taking up of his intel-lectual position. Greek intellectualism was too fortunate, too naïve, too aesthetic, too ironical, too spiritual ... too sinful to ever imagine that anyone could willingly and knowingly fail to do good or, knowing what was good, could willingly and knowingly do evil. No human being can by him-self and of himself define what sin is, precisely because he is in sin; all his talk about sin is basically a sinful covering-up. This is the reason why Christianity starts with another proposition, and that is that a revelation is needed from God in order to show man what sin is.[1]

In her proclamation, which is essentially gospel—good news—the church of Christ will thus also have to include exhortation, awakening a new *élan* and a more radical devotion to the service of one's fellow men.

According to the New Testament the Christian is someone who, being logically consistent, sins no more. For he has, as we say, 'received justice', he is

[1] J. Weterman, 'Macht en onmacht van de zonde naar het getuigenis van het N.T.', *Dux*, 28 (1962), 202.

a spiritual being, his body is a temple of the Holy Spirit, which he has received from the Lord and which lives in him. (See Rom 12: 9; 13: 10; 14: 15; 1 Cor 8: 1; 2 Cor 6: 6.) But the bible takes into account the possibility that the Christian may fall into sin. Although he is fundamentally freed from sin by his choice for Christ, he is not free from the possibility of sinning. Hence the ever-recurring exhortations to live a life that is true to one's calling. (See Rom 6: 3, 6: 8: 12–13, 24; Gal 5: 24.)

A human being is not finished once he has made his choice; he has still to grow towards the fullness of Christ, to make his conversion more deeply true in his life. The early church was very much aware that human life is threatened by egoism and laziness. That is why she speaks of the narrow gate and the weeds in the field (Mt 7: 13–14; 13: 36–43). But however plainly these admonitions may sound, one still doesn't get the impression that the New Testament considers it normal or customary for the Christian to live in separation from his Lord. Although Paul is acquainted with false apostles and false brethren (2 Cor. 11: 13–15, 26; Gal 2: 4), he certainly does not treat the majority of Christians as people who live sinful lives. The most frequently appearing faults seem to be those which do not exclude from the kingdom of heaven but which grieve, even though they do not drive out, the Holy Spirit (Eph 4: 30). From the preaching of Jesus handed down to us by the apostolic church we gather that man is more weak than sinful, needing salvation rather than refusing it. Christ lays charges only against those who pride themselves on their own perfection.

Now we must not rashly conclude from the above that according to Scripture good-yet-weak human beings 'therefore' never go as far as to sin seriously. It would, generally speaking, be unrealistic to expect it to give a precise explanation on gradations in sin. Anyone who is to any degree familiar with biblical thought knows that its approach is not primarily 'psychological' but 'existential'. The bible describes the lack of prospect and universality of sin in which humanity in general and each human being in particular find themselves, as long as they are untouched by the life of Jesus. Being a Christian demands a lasting effort, invites us to treat the beatitudes of the Sermon on the Mount and the parables of the kingdom as a never-reached, but continually-sought-after, ideal in our life. But the person who strives to this end in the strength and the example of Jesus Christ can also remember that God's love remains with him, that God's heart is more generous and more loving than the human beings before him can express. It is certain that in the preaching of the Lord we nowhere find that a breaking of the relationship with Love can 'suddenly' fall upon a person, that, as has more often been preached—wrongly—one moment is decisive for eternity. Here, in these human relations and limited earthly structures, one happening can have irreparable consequences for our whole future among human beings. But God's heart is more generous, his eye is sharper, and therefore more merciful.

Conversion to faith in the Father and to love for our fellow men

The extent to which the biblical summons to conversion concerns every one of us is perhaps most clearly seen when we look into the actual content of this idea. It does not so much imply the correcting of one or another element in our existence. It demands the real acceptance of a new and decisive message concerning our life, announced in the word and gesture of Jesus of Nazareth. We are thereby called to faith in Jesus' Father and love for our fellow men.

This is not something obvious and still less is it the work of one day. What is obvious to us is that others take an interest in us, that they give us support, that they are charitable when we have earned their criticism. Living faith and real love can only hesitatingly become the central intention of our life in a laborious and often painful process of growth.

It is already years since Bonhoeffer characterised the life and work of Jesus as a 'living-for-others', as a 'pro-existent' life: 'encounter with Jesus Christ implies the discovery that here the radical changing of human existence in its entirety takes place. For Jesus lives only for others. Believing means participating in this existence. Our relationship with God involves a new life of "pro-existence", of participation in Jesus' existence.'[1]

Conversion means henceforth not being captivated first and foremost by one's own need, anxiety and uncertainty, but allowing oneself to be carried along the path on which the Lord has preceded us, so that

[1] D. Bonhoeffer, *Letters and Papers from Prison*, Collins, London (1959).

messianic event may become reality in us and so that we may truly be the hand with which God cares for his creation. To the disciples of John the Baptist who come to ask if he is the one who is to come, God-with-us, Christ gives the answer: 'Go and tell John what you hear and see: the blind receive their sight and the lame walk, lepers are cleansed and the deaf hear, and the dead are raised up, and the poor have good news preached to them' (Mt 11: 4-5).

When someone lives like Jesus, he will recognise need and will try to be 'with' the other person. Those of us who have ever gone through loneliness and darkness know what a grace it was to meet a human being who listened and, by doing this, already offered new hope—someone who did not condemn, but understood and went further along the way with us, so that we were able to walk on once more. Seen in this way, salvation is in the first place the share that falls to us when we encounter a person who is for us what Christ was for his fellow men: 'He has borne our griefs and carried our sorrows' (Is 53: 4).

The call to conversion includes a call to fellowship

We tend to think at once of the word *conversion* as meaning primarily 'repenting and doing penance'. From what we have said above it will already be clear that this interpretation can hardly be called scriptural. In the bible inward conversion is indicated, the changing of mentality through which the whole range of human behaviour is involved. The Hebrew equivalent of this term expresses—according to the preposition used—the turning away from evil as well as the turning towards Yahweh.

Thus the first summons by Jesus, of which scripture speaks, certainly did not sound like a call to 'do penance in sackcloth and ashes'. To the Aramaic listeners it must have had above all the sound of glad tidings, gospel: now the time of salvation had dawned, the time of the great return. However, this message can only be accepted by the person who has had a concrete experience of the weakness of his own existence, of his inability to be perfect, and the continual need for forgiveness. Those who rely on their known achievements and are full of self-satisfaction thereby put a screen between themselves and Christ's message. The only person who can turn back is one who finds that he is never at rest as long as he is alone. The invitation to conversion can only be understood as gospel by those whose humble attitude singles them out as the poor in spirit and who do not expect salvation and peace to come from themselves but from another (and thus from the Other). The parables of the pharisee and the tax collector (Lk 18: 10–14), the prodigal son (Lk 15: 11–32), and the labourers in the vineyard (Mt 20: 1–16), are all meant to be accusations of self-satisfaction and presumption.

Therefore conversion does not have an intrinsically negative character. We are called to fellowship, —togetherness—with each other, to fellowship with God in Jesus. But this vocation will unavoidably bring pain and difficulty with it. Giving one's assent to what God expects of us, growing to Christ's standard in orientation towards others, is an everlasting task.

At the same time, human fellowship is not just a matter of self-sacrifice. Kwant expressed this exceptionally clearly a short while ago:

Naturally, in order to live in human fellowship we must abandon separate individual existence. We must live in the common interest and open out our separated interests to others. We do not throw ourselves open to the other person if we do not open our field of interest to him. There is thus an egoism which we must conquer in order to exist in human fellowship. From this point of view we may speak of self-abandonment. But this self-abandonment is to a great extent compensated by the fact that in human fellowship we rediscover ourselves in a new way. In human fellowship we become ourselves. This is simply the sensing, self-realisation, experiencing of value. It is not a self-sacrifice. We receive as much as we give, for in human fellowship not only does the other person become himself, but so do we. The sexual relationship is an outstanding example of this. The partners exist for each other but both achieve the fulfilment of their existence. Egoism and altruism cannot be completely separated here. They coincide in a higher unity.[1]

The personal character of conversion

The call to conversion applies to all human beings without exception, but will differ in tone according to the person to whom it is directed. We see this clearly in scripture. In the bible it is a less radical

[1] R. Kwant, 'Godsliefde en medemenselijkheid', *Tijdschrift voor Theologie*, 3 (1963), 274-5.

event for Ecclesiasticus than it is for Jeremiah. 'For there it was a question of all or nothing, there it was a fight for the preservation of faith in Yahweh; in the former case, however, that faith is supposed present but within the bounds of the recognition of Yahweh there remains room, from the moral point of view, for false steps and temporary aberration.'[1] We see the same thing in the preaching of the apostles; they generally presume that conversion is more radical for the heathen than for the Jew, who already has knowledge of the true God. To the converted Jews Paul emphasises the grace of God which can achieve all things and lets it be known 'that no man is justified before God by the law' (Gal 3: 11). Whereas he encourages the Greeks to renounce the false wisdom of the world which is folly with God (1 Cor 3: 19) and to believe in the crucified Christ, 'for the foolishness of God is wiser than men, and the weakness of God is stronger than men' (1 Cor 1: 25).

It is obvious that today also, in our world, similar differences in conversion will be present. We are not all in the same position, we do not all experience the same temptation.

Every choice in life must be remade

The first conversion takes place in baptism. Being baptised means choosing a life like that of Jesus: in faith, in devotion to the Father, in ready service of, and fellowship with, the human beings around us. Our task is to live a consistent life.

The particular nature of our human existence is

[1] A. Hulbosch, *De Bijbel over de bekering*, Roermond 1963), 28.

such that we can never express ourselves radically and definitively in one act. This could only happen in a complete, intuitive act into which our whole life would have to be compressed. Existing in the extension of time and space, we can only grow towards greater unity. As J. Walgrave said in an article in 1960, 'we must continually choose anew the basic direction of our life. It never stiffens into a habit. We always swerve into the other lane. In addition, our personality is only gradually made one and fitted into love's plan of service.'[1]

Is this not what every human being experiences? There is nothing that we can do once and for all, because in reality we never give ourselves totally but always bit by bit. We cannot do otherwise. Today we are generous, but tomorrow we back out shyly, perhaps only once more to struggle towards maximum effort in a few days or a week or so. This is the reality of the mutual relations between people, of the relationship of love between man and wife, of our experience of being a Christian. Again and again we climb to the heights of readiness to live for others, to see our occupation as a calling, to regard our marriage partner pre-eminently as the human person who is entrusted to us so that we may care for and bring happiness to him or her. But time and again we also fall down, we manipulate them in order to get our way and to make ourselves the centre of the world.

Our life swings high and low in continual commotion. We shall probably hardly be capable of

[1] J. Walgrave, 'Standpunten en stromingen in de hedendaagse moraal-theologie', *Tijdschrift voor Theologie*, I (1960), 60.

saying whether during the last two or three years we have reached a level from which we have never since descended. C. van Ouwerkerk points out: 'There are peaks, but also periods of humdrum routine; decline and revival alternate with each other, but their succession cannot be mapped out on a continuously ascending straight line. Only in their total context do events and periods say something about man, because as a whole they manifest the love of which a person—at any time in his life— was capable. Man is not totally himself at any given moment, he does not continually receive the chance of giving himself totally—and this is not necessary anyway. We are presenting a false ideal if we ask that man should continually be overtaxing himself.'[1]

We believe that, given these facts, the choice of our baptism must be remade, reaffirmed in our life. Not so much because it might be said that man has fallen from a previously attained height, but so that he may continue with renewed strength on the journey which leads through valleys and over hills and which is to bring him ultimately to the new Jerusalem, of which it is written: 'the dwelling of God is with men. He will dwell with them, and they shall be his people, and God himself will be with them; he will wipe away every tear from their eyes, and death shall be no more, neither shall there be mourning nor crying nor pain any more, for the former things have passed away' (Rev 21: 3–4).

In view of this human journey there is an intrinsic question to be asked concerning the 'second baptism', as the early church more often called the

[1] C. van Ouwerkerk, 'Christelijke levensgeschiedenis als genade', *Kerugma*, 6 (1963), 8 *n.* 4.

sacrament of penance. We shall speak in the following chapter about the form in which it should take place; at the moment we wish to establish whether it arises or not. We have to recognise our lack of radical reform, once more expressly confess our dependence on others—and, by doing this, our dependence on the Other who is God. In recognising the pettiness and bourgeois character of our life, forgiveness can once more be granted, together with the possibility of new love and security.

The eschatological direction of our conversion

Becoming a Christian means 'saying yes' to a life such as that which Christ led, engaging oneself in his service and that of the gospel, all of which will take place in the form of an individual calling which uses the opportunities a person has in his particular life. The conversion of which scripture speaks does not primarily consist in wanting to free oneself from one or other moral fault. In that case concern for self-perfection, lack of guilt and one's own happiness could easily predominate. It would be 'the completion of a task' from which self-control and a heavenly reward are expected—and probably also a murmur of approval from one's audience.

The Christian may not be a person who is anxiously worried about his own salvation or who 'obtains it'. If he wishes to be grasped to the very core of his personality by the Lord he will accept that the kingdom of God means, in the strict sense, willing for the world and its structures what God wills. For with the appearance of Christ the time is fulfilled and the kingdom of God near at hand; in him God is with us. The city of God about which the Book of Revelation speaks will indeed come down from on high as a gift of God, but it will at the same time be equally the result of our human activity. The world has been entrusted to us. Paul says of it: 'For the creation waits with eager longing for the revealing of the sons of God' (Rom 8: 19). We must work in order to make the world inhabitable for everyone, in order that we may live side by side; allaying sickness, suffering and even death as far as possible, in creating freedom and more loving fellowship.

Isaiah has evoked this new world for us: 'They shall build houses and inhabit them; they shall plant vineyards and eat their fruit. They shall not labour in vain, or bear children for calamity' (Is 65: 21, 23). This vision becomes reality where we live for each other and where we also see the sciences, economics and technology as the means of more deeply penetrating and more fully controlling the world and ourselves, so that true humanity may everywhere be made present.

In giving his attention to the world man must realise that the development of humanity is no uniform ascént, but a struggle. It is precisely as a Christian, experiencing how real the temptation towards a gain-seeking mentality can be, that man knows that as individual and as group he can abuse the power given him to complete the world into a community of love. It is in no way necessary that every century should show progress in humanity. The actual coming of the kingdom of God, the climbing of the human race towards a new heaven and a new earth, can be headed off by our freedom into lying, selfishness and hatred. 'Thus there can be no ultimate certainty for humanity that salvation is being realised, except in the promise of God that his grace conquers sin. If God were not triumphantly to realise his plan of salvation, even in opposition to the power of our wickedness, the great current of evolution could silt up into a desert of conflict, tyranny and pride.'[1]

The ethic of the New Testament is in the first place an ethic of intention

Many people consider confession as a sort of instrument for improvement, designed to help them overcome certain weaknesses and sins. It is in this way that they experience the phrase in the act of contrition whereby they resolve that they 'will not sin again'. When confession fails to 'work' as they had expected, their reaction is often one of discouragement.

It is noticeable, however, that scripture thinks of conversion in another way. Its intention is not that a sinful deed should call up a deed of compunction and penance in return. It places the accent elsewhere.

When we investigate the way in which the gospels describe sin we see that this is basically the sin of the unbelieving Jews: the voluntary, self-satisfied refusal to accept Jesus as the Messiah. If they had been blind, like the other sinners, then they would have been 'without guilt', for Jesus came into the world precisely in order to cure blindness (Jn 9). But because the Jewish leaders gave the pretence of being able to see, their guilt remains (Jn 9: 41).

[1] P. Smulders, 'Het christelijk evolutionisme van Teilhard de Chardin', *Nederlandse katholieke Stemmen*, 59 (1963), 157.

Here we seem to be touching on the essence of sin, which should be seen most clearly in those who received Jesus' sharpest criticism: 'Thus the New Testament often speaks of sin as unbelief. This is essentially the same thing as not allowing oneself to be helped, to be loved. Unbelief is the refusal to entrust oneself to him who reveals himself in Jesus. It contains elements of pride, the urge for autonomy. Thus unbelief means at the same time rebellion, revolt against him who manifests himself as the Lord of my life.'[1] From Jesus' attitude, from the way in which he reacts, we see that individual sins fade away before the fundamental one. We must even say that the experience of one's own insufficiency and sinfulness, of one's need of the other person and his love, forms a favourable disposition for the reception of Christ's message. An *individual sin* can be said to have a double significance: it can—when one experiences it as sinful— cause a growth in the longing to be in fellowship with others. It can also be the sign of a decisive choice against Christ.

That which we meet in scripture we also discover once more in our own lives. Beneath all the external identity between two acts an enormous difference in meaning can be present. Two people can do precisely the same thing, whilst it is *not* the same thing in each case. We partially express this insight in the words we use. Killing someone and murdering them is not the same thing. It *is* something entirely different, even though this difference need not be visible in the outward activity which realises the event. Saying something which is not true is not always a

[1] Weterman, 204.

case of lying. A kiss can be the expression of sympathy or love, but it can also be the sign of the traitor. And without wishing to pass judgement in the question of marital relations, we may say that every concrete method of birth-regulation can be motivated by egoism and shortsightedness, but also by real concern for family and marriage partner. Even here no method is simply good or simply bad. Outwardly the same operation, the removal of a healthy kidney, can in one case be an aimless mutilation and in another—that of transplantation—a deed of love and human fellowship *par excellence*.

Far too little attention is paid to this fact, at least in the practice of moral judgement. Here 'measuring up the act as it stands', establishing with a photographic objectivity 'what is taking place' has had and continues to have clear priority over the question 'what is this person really trying to do?', 'what is the significance of his action?', 'what does it mean in the context of his life, with its past and its future?', 'what does it mean for others; does it build up or disrupt the community?'. We must constantly bear in mind that our human activity is essentially intersubjective. Furthermore, we may not cut this activity up into small pieces so as to then study each piece separately, making abstraction, moreover, of the living intention of the person acting.[1]

A person can succumb to temptation and unlaw-

[1] In this connection we would refer the reader to W. van der Marck's exposition of the essential intersubjectivity of human activity in his *Love and Fertility*, Sheed and Ward, London (1965), especially pp. 52–5.

fully appropriate something. He can also have a dishonest attitude in business matters. Every one of us knows that there are days when our work fails to run smoothly, when we allow ourselves to be too easily distracted or just let the time pass by idly; this experience is also gone through by the person who seriously and devotedly achieves the task entrusted to him, thereby distinguishing himself from the loafer and layabout.

Our deeds are not things which can be weighed and measured in a purely objective manner. Certainly, they do have an objective aspect and the general estimation of the sinfulness of a deed is the elaboration of this aspect. But our deeds are in the first place personal. This is not a question of additional, subjective considerations, it is their first and most essential property. They receive and manifest their moral value, positive or negative, only within the total plan of life, the total orientation of a person's life and within the total internal and external situation—that is to say, the situation created by his emotional temperament and the concrete circumstances in which the action takes place.

The positive or negative moral value of our deeds must be judged in the light of the fundamental moral orientation of our person. Just as the moral life of the good man forms a unity through the taking up and streamlining of all expressions of life into the movement of love, so there is also a unity in immoral life.[1]

[1] Walgrave, 59.

It is not to be denied that even with all the hesitation and lack of consistency which can be present in a person's life, there still exists a certain basic structure. Ultimately there are two possibilities in our choice of life. We can choose a life of goodness, generosity, dedication, a life of existence for others. We can also refuse this most profound vocation which is our common calling, see our existence as an existence for ourself and manipulate others as we manipulate something which is at our disposal.

In the measure that an action, a life, is inspired by the intention to love, it is good and virtuous. In the measure that an attitude, a deed is determined by a struggle for power, domination and manipulation, that life is a sinful one. As Walgrave says, 'Pride is not one sin among others, just as love is not one virtue among others. Pride is the *forma* of all sin, the *choix original* of all sinful existence. A deed is sinful, in the strict sense of that word, to the extent that our human pride is invested in it. Naturally, one can describe the permanent qualities of behaviour governed by pride: lust for power, cruelty, doing evil to others, sensual egoism, and so on; and thus we rediscover all the various sins as varying forms in which pride embodies itself in the diverse situations of life and with regard to particular problems.'[1]

We are now perhaps in a better position to understand the reaction of Jesus to the pharisees' blind adhesion to the law and overestimation of works, as also to the sinfulness of so many of the poor in spirit. An essential element of conversion and thus of

[1] Walgrave, 59.

repentance can now help us to see the problem more clearly.

When the Lord denounces the piety of the pharisee his rejection is not of real piety but of its inauthentic practice, of the false attitude which factually underlies it. It is he who sees into the heart of man; the intention which can remain hidden for us external spectators now becomes manifest. 'Previously it had not yet been known what was hiding beneath that upper layer of an awareness in which sin and conversion took place. It was not generally known that underneath there slumbered a self-satisfaction, attachment to which attached one to sin.'[1]

Christ saw through the external facade. He saw what a person was really doing, searching for, and trying to manifest, in his life. For this reason his judgement was—and is—often so different from that of those who wield an external criterion, which they call objective. According to the Gospel of John, people were divided around Jesus, the Light and Life of the world, into those who believed and those who refused to do so. A division takes place, but it is a division which consists of a process of crystallisation around Christ.

Henceforth we know that God does not judge us on outward behaviour, but on what goes on in our heart. We believe that we are on the way towards him in the measure that we sincerely try to give expression to love in the various fields of our existence (1 Jn 4: 12). When, in doing this, we continually experience our weakness, our need of forgiveness, then perhaps we understand better the

[1] Hulbosch, 62.

petition of the tax collector: 'God, be merciful to me a sinner', and also Jesus' statement 'this man went down to his house justified rather than the other' (Lk 18: 14).

The chasm between *willing* and *being able to*, between *heart* and *act*, which runs through our life can, on the basis of this knowledge, be bridged, at least in principle. But it will remain present in our life, often in a painful way. We all so often fail to succeed. Real progress can seldom be noted. Much remains unattainable for us. Certainly we prepare ourselves, but when the moment comes we are often dragged under by impatience, weariness and desire. This often disappoints us in our daily life; every sincere person will find it a pity, but if he is sensible he will recognise how unavoidable it all is. We must take this into account when judging ourselves and, just as much, when judging others. God sees into our heart. He knows the direction in which we are groping our way. For this reason his charity is itself justice.

Conversion and repentance are much more than knowing oneself to be guilty in this or that event, than being sorry about this or that deed and 'trying to make up for the wrong done'. This was done also by the pharisee. He even fasted twice in the week and was still neither able nor willing to enter the kingdom of heaven. Nor does repentance mean regretting that things have not worked out differently. It consists in a sincere, everyday effort to 'put on Christ', to let one's life be inspired by human fellowship, to come basically to grips with the inconsistencies which result from our eternal wavering between ourself and others. We are deceiving ourselves, as Rahner rightly remarks,[1] if we think that we are regretting a lack of love when we merely make an act of contrition, say a Hail Mary as penance, and leave everything else just as it was, without asking pardon from the person we caused pain. Why do we act as if we are repenting of something which we cannot or do not wish to change at all? We must learn to feel our way to the depths, to see through the external appearance of our life to that which actually moves us.

Whilst in imitation of the preaching of Jesus Christ we recognise the ethical primacy of a person's intention, this does not mean we fail to appreciate the primary significance of external actions. It is a fact that the outward act both reveals and at the same time conceals our deeper moral choice. To those who pay close attention a person reveals himself by what he does, even when he does not wish to reveal himself, when his action is not an honest reflection of his actual choice. But his activity equally conceals this choice, if only for the reason that because of the 'resistance of the world' we shall never completely succeed in translating our intentions into deeds—not only for this reason, however, but also for the reason that one and the same outward event can, as we have pointed out already, have a variety of meanings. Thus we readily agree with Schoonenberg when he writes:

It is certainly misleading to say of a specific

[1] Karl Rahner, 'Beichtprobleme', in *Schriften zur Theologie*, vol. III, Benziger, Einsiedeln (1956), 236. Volumes I, II and V are available in English under the title *Theological Investigations* (London and Baltimore, 1961ff.).

external action 'this is a mortal sin' or 'that is a venial sin', or even to speak of an 'obligation under mortal sin' in the case of a positive law.[1]

Although on the one hand an action can be considered as a (not always trustworthy) sign of our inward intention, on the other hand it connotes an intervention in the world outside and within us.

Whatever a person does always has the character of a dialogue: it reveals the influence of and has repercussions upon the community of which he is a part, and on those with whom he lives, whether directly by what he does or says in their presence, or indirectly through his so-called private acts, thoughts, and feelings which will soon determine his attitude and his actions.[2]

Without being expressly aware of it, we are made richer or poorer by our activity. We grow through giving and devoting ourselves. We diminish by thinking of ourselves too much and by seeking our own advantage. We influence the world in which our neighbour lives: we make it either inhabitable and secure, or hard and inhospitable.

Grades in personal sin: venial, serious, and mortal, sin[3]

In the practice of Christian life questions concerning

[1] Piet Schoonenberg, SJ, *Man and Sin*, Sheed and Ward, London (1965), 36.
[2] van der Marck, 53.
[3] For this exposition we owe much to the contributions of P. Schoonenberg, in *Man and Sin*, 25–40, and of C. Anderson in *De Bazuin*, 44 (1960–61), *n*. 24. Although we differ from both of these writers on certain points, in this matter we feel ourselves to be of very much the same opinion.

gradation in personal sin have long played a great role. We have already indicated that scripture does not arrive at a sharply defined teaching on this point. Of ancient tradition we may see that it was aware of two things: it recognised that we all fall short daily, but that this does not imply that we are therefore unworthy of celebrating the eucharist and receiving the body of the Lord. It likewise recognised that there are Christians who because of their behaviour may not participate in this celebration.

If we try to see some sort of order in the subsequent development of tradition, we sometimes notice a tendency really only to look towards God when establishing 'degrees' of sin. Distinctions are made more or less exclusively dependent on God's arbitrary decision, which punishes certain deeds with the loss of eternal life and not others. Most theologians have constantly maintained the conviction, however, that God takes his creation seriously. For this reason they have tried to define degrees of sin on the basis of the nature and significance of the act in question, together with its proper character as human activity. Hence they arrive at the view that what is really completely contrary to God's law must be designated mortal sin and that what is not so much against the law, but consists more or less in 'getting round the law', is venial sin. In its heart, moral theology has always known that it must pay attention primarily to the depth of human self-expression. That is why it has always held that any 'matter' can be the object of mortal sin.

It is equally true that pastoral practice often demands a clear and handy rule. Stealing one shilling is clearly a different matter from taking a hundred pounds: the former occurs more 'easily', it usually demands less consideration, and does not weigh so heavily on a person's conscience; it happens somewhat less noticeably and in most cases requires no deep decision. This truth was then generalised: certain actions were labelled 'mortal sins' and others 'venial sins', on the basis of the degree of inward intention which might reasonably be supposed in normal circumstances.

The subjective ground (the inward decision) and the objective ground (the externally visible seriousness of the action in question) were often placed side by side in judging the degree of sin. Thus the Dutch catechism of 1948 reads, in reply to questions 284 and 287:

> We commit mortal sin if we transgress the law of God in an important matter with full knowledge and completely free will. We commit venial sin if we transgress the law of God in a small matter, or if we transgress God's law in an important matter, but without full knowledge or complete free will.

And of course we have all been taught that certain things are 'mortal sins' and others 'venial sins'.

It is our firm contention that 'measuring the act as it stands' cannot be considered before or apart from an understanding of a person's moral intention. It must therefore be recognised that we cannot have at our disposal constant, cut-and-dried criteria which provide more-or-less handy and sharply defined boundaries and gradations in sinfulness. As an ecclesial science, moral theology knows that its

72

duty is, whilst sensing and feeling for the meaning of our human existence, to express in words God's expectation and intentions with regard to human life for every generation and culture. But in doing this it must remember Bonhoeffer's statement:

> An ethic cannot be a book in which there is set out how everything in the world actually ought to be but unfortunately is not, and an ethicist cannot be a man who always knows better than others what is to be done and how it is to be done. An ethic cannot be a work of reference for moral action which is guaranteed to be unexceptional, and an ethicist cannot be the competent critic and judge of every human activity.[1]

Let us begin by looking for a principle of the various ways in which man can come to sin. According to contemporary philosophical expression the physical aspect of my being constitutes the transition from the conscious ego to the world. It is the reality which 'grafts' me to things. It is my body that assures my being-in-the-world, that involves me in the world, that gives me a position in it. So I discover myself as existing in the world, in the extension of time and space, with past and future, with possibilities about which I can dream and within that limitation which makes me always one human being in one situation. I live and am continually carried on afresh, I 'am lived'; I discover perhaps only afterwards how much my so-called choice is determined by emotions and impulses which arise from my situation and my temperament and which are conditioned by the toughness of reality within and outside me. The

[1] D. Bonhoeffer, *Ethics*, Glasgow (1964), 269.

world, the people around me, carry me along with them, shape me and call on me to answer. And I answer in fact: I am continually taking up an attitude. Often I can only afterwards see what it actually was. Sometimes I am more or less aware at the moment itself that I must give an answer. Then I can perhaps perceive continuous lines in my life and see to some degree whether my life is in fact moving in the direction of love and growing generosity. But no human being is really competent to judge, not even to judge himself. In this respect he must make Paul's words his own: 'I am not aware of anything against myself, but I am not thereby acquitted. It is the Lord who judges me. Therefore do not pronounce judgement before the time, before the Lord comes, who will bring to light the things now hidden in darkness and will disclose the purposes of the heart. Then every man will receive his commendation from God' (1 Cor 4: 4–5).

Following on from the description given above, we can state the following: every human being carries out actions which more or less escape him and actions in which he determines himself by his own choice. The former we may call hidden, impersonal deeds and the latter personal deeds. In the reality of life the distinction between the two categories is fluid; in general, sharp boundaries cannot be drawn. It is a question of 'more or less'. According to the measure of human self-expression which underlies them, we should like to call the choice of evil which takes place in these deeds venial sin or serious sin.

Venial sin is already partly contained in the limited, not yet balanced and integrated person who we are; again and again we have to admit to ourselves that we are seeking the easy way out and are so inconsiderate that we are irritable and curt. Every person knows of his own accord how much he still needs to grow towards more mature and more charitable humanity.

We use the term *serious sin*, and do not speak of mortal sin, precisely because here it is still a question of decisions which are taken in an instant, on an impulse. We seriously object to the suggestion that life-deciding mortal sin might be located in one detached deed, seen atomistically, on its own. The nature peculiar to human existence is precisely such that we can never determine ourselves in one detached deed. Thus also in moral judgement the emphasis needs to be laid upon a man's design in life, the design in life which causes me to become myself in wishing to be with the other person, or which enslaves me to freely chosen self-alienation in isolation. Mortal sin is always the result of something, it presupposes a growth and development. Hereby we do not wish to deny that there are moments in which we experience ourselves as being placed before a choice. However, when within a fundamentally virtuous plan of life the choice turns out to be a negative one we then speak of serious sin and of nothing more than that. We only wish to call *mortal sin* that which really separates man from love. For as long as we continue to use this term equally for 'momentary', 'loose' deeds we shall continue to further a development of conscience which cannot be called healthy. Then we shall also continue to hear the remark: 'It's a bit hard that you get punished for eternity if after a good life you "happen" to fall into mortal sin and die in that state.'

Certainly, within a fundamentally good direction someone can take on the attitude of a serious sinner. He can clearly go against his conscience, forget his place in the personal community. Then he will drag another into his particular world in order to subject him to it. In this case love does not seek its way with zeal, but is eliminated by selfish desire.

Nevertheless, the great difference from the fundamentally wrong attitude to life is that the possibility described above is a passing situation, a 'detached' deed. It is kicking over the traces, not actually being oneself. For this reason the person will want to 'make good' his offence: he is 'not really like that' and therefore returns to himself. Not returning, not retracing one's steps, not fighting to do so, after the fascination of the moment and the confusion of the situation, can precisely be a sign that it was not a question of kicking over the traces, but the expression, the birth, or confirmation, of a negative attitude.

In sin man expresses himself as being against his neighbour, thus against God, with whom he is called to be in community. How does sin take place in this relation? Take marriage, for example.

Love for each other naturally does not exclude our often causing each other pain, being inconsiderate, taking the justified desires of the other too little into account, not living on the level of Christ's love. These imperfections and this falling short form the venial sins.

It is possible that in a normal, healthy marriage a deep insult to one partner may occur, a deed which is in fierce opposition to love and through which the husband or wife at this particular moment is clearly given second place. Must it now be accepted that a deep relationship between two people who try to be really good to one another is *immediately* shattered by a deed which goes against it? It sometimes seems so, but then looking more closely the deed which breaks the bond of union is seen to be the expression of an attitude and shows the insulted partner clearly that he or she had actually been deceived for quite some time. Even if the insulting deed were to be adultery, it does not immediately break up the marriage. If the other partner sees—and this is often extremely difficult—that it really was a foolish whim on the part of the other, but no more than that, then not only is forgiveness made possible but, in spite of great disappointment, the community of love is preserved in its essence from *both* sides. With neither of them is there a moment of breaking, of real separation. People grow towards one another: they also grow apart.

By speaking in this way we do not wish to minimise sin. We believe that man chooses good and chooses evil. But this choice of life only apparently takes place at clearly defined moments. A choice of life becomes continually transformed. Particular events have their own very great significance in the realisation of this choice. Mortal sin, which really and definitively separates man from God's love—unless a miracle of grace takes place— does not suddenly fall out of the sky. It is made possible through laxity, through being satisfied with the minimum.

3
Liturgical and extra-liturgical forgiveness of sin

The secularisation of ethics: God withdraws from the world

In the film *The Ten Commandments* there is a detailed picture of Yahweh giving Moses the Ten Commandments. Israel is grouped anxiously around the foot of Mount Sinai. Moses stands high up on the mountain. Amid thunder and lightning the words of God's law are blazed into pillars of rock.

It was in this way that earlier popular representation saw it: God gives the law, he promulgates commandments in a clear manner. The prophet stands between God and the people; he transmits the will of the Creator, he threatens the people with punishment and entices them with reward. In this world God is close by: he speaks in thunder and lightning. He also abides with his people at night in the heavenly constellations, he gives fertility to man, beast and plant. When his people is unfaithful to him he strikes it with sickness or with drought. Returning to his merciful disposition, he grants a cure and lets there be rain for the earth. The man of God prays. He withdraws from the pressure of human existence, climbs the mountain in order to be with God and through his prayer to receive the real blessing of the Lord.

Almost without it having been noticed, our world has grown out of this way of thinking of God. The idea of a continually intervening God, who with his laws regulates our life as if from without, who rewards with the full harvest and punishes with floods—this idea strikes us as somewhat primitive. We have come to feel at home in this world, we are continually discovering more about its internal structures. Much of what seemed to be the work of God's hand can now be performed or at least predicted by modern man. We no longer encounter God, in this sense, in our lives, as was certainly still the case a few generations ago. Having become independent and conscious of our own strength, we also accept less and less that our lives should be ruled by norms which come from without.

This process we designate by the term *desacralisation*. Whilst in former times everything was in fact mysterious, brought about by the gods and eternally ordained, today man forms an idea of events, discovers uniformity, he knows what is reasonably possible and impossible. Is not modern science convinced that in the foreseeable future it will be able to make certain weather forecasts, regulate the climate, and even arrive at the automatic diagnosis of symptoms of disease? That which was mysterious in earlier times, a sign from heaven, the expression of God's unfathomable decree, has now become the symptom of something which the medical man can diagnose and predict, or of which the meteorologist can tell the cause and further development. A great advantage can lie in this process of desacralisation: man can really take hold of the course of history and dominate the whims of climate and season. But it also remains possible that man may forget that his power is a gift, that his world is a creation, that his destiny lies in being together with others in the Lord. Aldous Huxley's visions of the future in *Brave New World* and George Orwell's in *Nineteen eighty-four* paint us pictures of the world which arise as a result of the tendency to spend every moment of the day as efficiently as possible, to obtain greater and greater prosperity, and to let not a single moment be lost in actually reflecting upon the meaning of human existence.

God is withdrawing from the world. Is he being thought of as the ever-silent, ever-absent one? It might also be true that our image of him is becoming less tangible, but growing in completeness. Our conception of his providence is changing, but not becoming less authentic. We believe in his care just as we believe in miracles. There undeniably occur many miracles of goodness and love in our world, for many people are truly good to one another. God has entrusted the world to us. He cares for us through other people just as he sends us out to make others our neighbour and to bring about a miracle of love. Divine providence and human prediction do not stand over and against each other. On the contrary, in the one we must experience the other. In our care for others we are God's hand. In the harshness of our lives, in sickness, in misunderstanding, we feel how little permeated by redemption this world still is.

Experience of God and experience of sin are available to us to the extent that we live in the atmosphere of God. We must develop in ourselves the sense of experiencing the Lord's presence in the world, of knowing ourselves to be supported by the caring providence which he shows us in the attitude of the person who loves us and whose care for us unites us both. For it was in this way that we learned to pray. When a child has had an enjoyable game or a satisfying meal, he can thank the Lord for it. He will say 'thank you very much' to Jesus for having a father and mother and for being able to receive their care as a matter of course. He learns to say 'Father', because he has a father who can do everything, upon whose knee he can sit and who carries him shoulder-high to bed.

Being present in and to this world, we are with God. Or, to put it the other way round, and thus more accurately: being present in and to this world, God is with us. Religiosity is above all the experiencing of the dimension of depth in our lives, of God's intimate presence.

If we are obedient to the guidance of the Spirit a new idea of God can indeed grow within us, that of the transcendent God, limited neither by nor to anything, who for this reason is present throughout the world, who is active in all our activity, who invites us through all being. When the God of intervention makes way for the Creator who is at work in all things and all people, then also will the God of regulations disappear before the God who calls upon us in all that exists; then, too, behind the neighbour in

whose regard we feel guilty there will rise for us
his Creator and Father.[1]

Secularisation in sin leads to secularisation in forgiveness

The development sketched above carries further
consequences. Just as we experience that we insult
God in our fellow men, so we also experience that
he forgives us in the forgiveness we receive from one
another. We are slowly but surely beginning to
believe that grace and thus forgiveness come to us
in the form of human fellowship. As Anderson says,
'In the concrete, God's grace, God's saving love
comes to man in and through human brotherly
love.' We can no longer deny the correctness of this
statement. Sin, which is a religious category, presupposes guilt, a human category. God is never the
only party to whom we have to account for ourselves; it is to man in the first instance. In him
God addresses us. Only in humanity does he come
to us, in his son Jesus Christ, in our neighbour in
whom Christ speaks to us. Already Moses, in his
day, longed to see Yahweh. But Moses was a man
and no man can see the face of God. We see his face
through the veil of creation. Our every approach to
him is an approach in and with human beings who
speak to us of him, who render him visible. We pray
in and through Jesus the Lord.

In the New Testament we read: 'You shall love

[1] Piet Schoonenberg, *De Macht der Zonde*, 's-Hertogenbosch (1962[4]), 42–3. The English translation of this
work already cited (*Man and Sin*, Sheed and Ward, London
[1965]) was extensively revised by the author, and does not
contain this passage.

the Lord your God with all your heart, and with all your soul, and with all your mind. This is the great and first commandment. And a second is like it, You shall love your neighbour as yourself' (Mt 22: 37–39). It is of paramount importance to see clearly that it is not here a question of two commandments which function more or less independently of one another. Love of God and human love are not alternatives, they coincide. The characteristic task of Christianity is that of passing on, of making tangible, the love of God, which comes upon us in a visible and humanly comforting way in Christ, God-with-us, and in all who live in imitation of Jesus. What God asks is the fulfilment of his goodness in the creature itself. God does not compete with man. That which we truly give him does not lessen our efforts on behalf of our fellow men. He never calls us away from another, but sends us out to make the other person our neighbour. This also means that we can never speak of sin which is directed *only* against God and which might be distinguishable from sin *directly* against man. Wherever we go against another and against ourself, we touch God, the origin and source of our existence, who calls upon us to fulfil our task in the world faithfully. When we forget that God is the Lord of our life, when we no longer turn back to him with thanks and praise and have no eye for the mystery of all that is, then we also violate our human existence, which is a gift, and we make ourselves inwardly incapable of achieving authentic humanity.

We must not set ourselves in opposition to secularisation in forgiveness. It would be a useless opposition, directed against one of the consequences of the growing maturity of man. Neither may we call this phenomenon as such a weakening of an awareness of sin. For, after all, we do not speak of a lack of faith in divine providence in a person who builds dikes to protect his land against the effects of autumn storms or who vaccinates his cattle in order to guard them against sickness.

The duty towards mutual reconciliation

'So if you are offering your gift at the altar, and there remember that your brother has something against you, leave your gift there before the altar and go; first be reconciled to your brother, and then come and offer your gift' (Mt 5: 23–24). In a changed conception of sin great attention must clearly be paid to this summons by Jesus. *Where we have offended, there we must also acknowledge our guilt and ask for forgiveness.* Our good relations with God cannot be restored unless—at least from our side—good relations are restored with the other person. 'Everyone knows how extremely hard it can be to approach a fellow human being who is perhaps most uncongenial, to whom one is going to acknowledge one's guilt and of whom one intends to ask forgiveness. Confessing to a non-involved third person, an affable pastor, is not so hard as confessing to someone who has a certain right to condemn.'[1]

Naturally, there can arise circumstances through which we are released from this confession of guilt. If a person is ignorant of the fact that he has harmed another, and would not even understand the nature of his offence if told, he cannot be expected to be contrite, nor should he be told of his

[1] P. Roscam Abbing, 40.

offence. Normally one's request for forgiveness can be made in various ways, depending on the situation in which the people concerned find themselves and upon the signs with which they express their mutual relationship. A gesture of friendliness or consideration, a service offered, can already contain an appeal for restoration of what was lost. The duty to acknowledge one's guilt to one's fellow men can be hard and difficult, but we should not run away from it. This should be clearly indicated in preaching. What we can be sure of is that God's heart is greater and more generous than that of our neighbour. Even when another person rejects us God's grace and forgiveness are present. A hand is never held out in vain.

The place for liturgical forgiveness of sins

One question now unavoidably presents itself. What is the point of liturgical forgiveness of sins if our guilt is removed in a reconciliation sought on the human level? When God accepts us lovingly once again through asking each other for forgiveness, what is there to be achieved in a liturgical celebration—without entering into considering what form such a celebration should take?

In a very recent article Müller says: 'The church's announcement is not a statement that sin has already previously been forgiven in private, but is an efficacious sign of the divine forgiveness which is taking place here and now.' We cannot entirely agree with this approach. Here liturgical forgiveness, which is pronounced in the sacrament of penance, is in fact isolated from the extra-liturgical, but without doubt is already an intrinsically ecclesial event which takes place in mutual reconciliation. On the other hand, the Dutch bishops rightly remarked in their pastoral letter on penance and forgiveness: 'From of old the church has acknowledged with scripture that there exist many forms of forgiveness of sin, liturgical and extra-liturgical, which do not stand in each others' way, but which precisely refer to each other: the sincere celebration of the eucharist, the silent prayer of repentance, fasting and almsgiving, the acknowledgement of guilt and the asking of forgiveness from one's neighbour. All these are, as it were, embraced and confirmed by the forgiveness which the priest pronounces in the sacrament of confession.'[1]

The question concerning the sense of liturgical forgiveness of sin is not a new one. Tradition also knew it, and scholasticism expressly occupied itself with the question as to why the man who had already received forgiveness for his serious sin must still go to confession.

We shall introduce our reply with a quotation from Schillebeeckx:

> . . . in the natural order, alongside the decisive and central acts of life, there are everyday actions which call for a personal involvement of a lesser kind. In the same way there are decisive Christian acts and everyday ones. . . . That which is lived out in an everyday manner outside the sacraments grows to its full maturity in them (this, at least, is the purpose of the sacramental system of salvation). Seen from Christ's point of view the sacraments are the express taking-hold of the man

[1] Pastoral Letter of the Dutch Bishops on penance and forgiveness, 16 March, 1965.

who receives them, because they are the earthly manifestation of the heavenly act of redemption. But the response to Christ's willing availability in encounter must therefore grow in the recipient to a culminating point which is personal and decisive. It is partly on human grounds that this response is possible, since the recipient realises his desire for grace in the visibility of the church. . . . The supremely important character of the sacraments derives from the fact that they bring a person's desire for grace to ecclesial manifestation. So through the sacraments the individual's desire for grace is linked with the redemptive power of that mystical body which is one with Christ. Again they are culminating moments because they are a special divine contact with a person in a situation which, for the Christian view of life, is decisive.[1]

We believe that Schillebeeckx' approach is fundamentally correct and can serve as a starting-point for the further development of our theme.

Let us commence with the marital situation. In a harmonious marriage man and wife know they are living for each other and for their family. They know this even when the pressures of day-to-day routine prevent them being specifically conscious of it. The relationship of love is constantly present and colours all their activities. The love of his wife helps a man to get through his often dull work day by day. He knows what he is ultimately working for. His wife knows this also and can therefore usually summon up the strength to make the beds with

[1] E. Schillebeeckx, *Christ the Sacrament*, 245–7.

care, do the washing, and keep the house tidy. Here, two people are living in an atmosphere of solidarity, whilst the moments when they are directly occupied with each other are probably quite infrequent. They live for each other, but this 'being-for-each-other' largely forms a hidden background against which their lives are led. In such a marriage, spontaneous 'celebrations' arise, moments in which all that was so unnoticed but present in a very real way is clearly expressed, is brought from the background into the foreground of experience. Thus a celebration is only authentic and true when it makes explicit that which is *real*, yet hardly consciously present. Neither experiences compete with each other: they presuppose one another and refer precisely to one another.

Our intention will now be clear. The truth about our existence is that we must, at one and the same time, both be ourselves, standing in earthly relationships, and experience ourselves and all our doings as totally 'of God'. In him we live, we move, we are. Our life is completely dependent on, and thus basically attached to, God. Every human being who is trying to be a Christian knows this. At certain moments he succeeds in experiencing his life in this way. Then he can spontaneously thank the Lord for the gift given him in human form. Christ was the man who was completely pure and therefore transparent to God. He also saw his Father veiled in the other person.

God must be the One we discover in and beneath our human coexistence, the source of all the good we experience when we gratefully enjoy the gifts of the world. We realise this so seldom. Because in everyday reality the redemptive significance of the profane is so inadequately experienced, we are in need of explicit celebrations. What Sonnen says in a discussion on Robinson's *Honest to God* has a wider application: 'In that case we are deeply made aware of the fact that the day now coming to a close has achieved for us a chapter in the history of salvation; we consciously receive this salvation and thank God for it, we acknowledge before God that our answer of love still falls short, and therefore ask forgiveness.'[1]

We must strive towards making a complete identity between the profane and the sacred sectors of our lives, so that we may be aware of the intrinsically sacred character of all our secular activities. We experience how difficult this is, how great our distance from the ultimate fulfilment in which we shall exist wholly for each other and at the same time be, and experience ourselves as being, totally with God. It is precisely because our relation to God remains to such a degree *only* a background experience, because we so seldom make ourselves aware of the way in which he grasps us in the person who cares for us, that we need celebrations in which we express how much he seeks us in the routine of everyday life. Liturgical celebration can cause us to become somewhat more strongly aware of his continual presence the whole day through, 'just as' the celebration of a wedding anniversary can have the effect that two people, who know in their hearts that they are living for each other, will more spontaneously make this basic experience into everyday

[1] R. Sonnen, 'Wereldse heiligheid', *Verbum* 31 (1964), 163. .

reality. Thus we understand Schillebeeckx' statement that the sacramental encounter with Christ is the moment of explicitation which throws into relief that which is so concealed and unnoticed.

Perhaps now it has become clearer why we laid so much emphasis in the first chapter upon the desirability of personal pastoral care in the administering of this sacrament. This is a necessary requirement for us to be able to speak of a *privileged action* and an *accentuated grasping*.

It is at least probable that many may not feel the need for such a celebration. In their case it is worth while reflecting on the reason why this need is not present. Is their life in fact so transparent to God that in the joy of inter-human reconciliation they already experience the nearness of God, who achieves everything? In missing this joy, because contact with their neighbour cannot be restored, do they desire the presence of Someone who 'will wipe away every tear' (Rev 21 : 4)? Or, with the secularisation of ethics, has God withdrawn from their life? For the naturally ambiguous event of desacralisation can, on the one hand, lead to a purifying of our idea of God, but on the other—as may be seen in practice—it can also hinder our very faith in God, our living in his continual presence. Can we not say that precisely because we no longer encounter him now in such a palpable way, we ought to search for him more?

Perhaps celebration can become superfluous because we continually experience God in the reality of our secular existence. But it may also be because he has disappeared even from the background of our life. According to our personal experience, there are always two spheres in our human existence: one profane and one sacred. To quote Sonnen once more: 'They coincide in reality and also in our intuition . . . we exist as pilgrims on this earth, as human beings for whom the holiness of the city of God without a temple is still only a promise; is not the tragic aspect of this existence of ours that we can never experience both of them in one act? The vitality of direct contact with reality in our profane, everyday existence lacks the depth in which to behold God, whereas kneeling at prayer in a church we do find this depth; although even there our experience remains somewhat abstract since it is the depth of something which we experienced elsewhere.'[1] Perhaps this is putting the matter a little too poignantly. There are moments when we touch on that unity. We must hope that they will become more and more numerous. But for most of us it is true to say that in order for us to experience God's generosity in the charity of human beings more deeply we need the explicitness of a celebration.

During the last few decades more attention has once more been given in the theology of penance to the ecclesial dimension of sin and reconciliation. Beemer rightly comments that this preaching has hardly found any acceptance with the majority of the faithful: 'This is probably connected with the fact that the experience of faith is still so much engrossed in struggling free from legalism and moralism and is as yet fully occupied in developing in the direction of increasing personalisation.'[2] We

[1] Sonnen, 164.
[2] Beemer, 284.

speak—or are spoken to—in an atmosphere which is often orientated towards a church of law, and we do not experience ourselves as *ecclesia*. Thus we bypass the fact that by his sin the baptised Christian makes himself guilty towards the church, the living bearer of God's loving mercy and care for people. In fact we know how much we are sometimes hurt by the church, how difficult it often is for us to experience her as the mother of all the faithful. But we knock against each other and make ourselves guilty towards each other when we remain below our capability of imitating the Lord. Christ made the most extreme self-surrender 'that he might present the church to himself in splendour, without spot or wrinkle or any such thing, that she might be holy and without blemish' (Eph 5: 27).

Thus it is a good thing to come together as a community, as the local church, with our desire of perfection, in order to acknowledge our guilt with regard to one another, if only by our presence and inward assent. For a public confession seems impracticable. It would in most cases be too heavy a demand, on the person in question as much as on the congregation of the faithful. Nor is it so important whether we confess particular incidents aloud or not; what is important is that through our attitude we should acknowledge our joint guilt for the situation which we are all constantly regretting. As long as we do not find doing this a matter of course we shall continue to experience the church as an association to which we belong in order to obtain better chances for our soul and sanctity.[1]

[1] Here we refer to what was said in chapter 2 under the heading *Every choice in life must be remade*.

The experience of grace in the liturgical forgiveness of sin

The journey to the confessional is painful and hard for many because they experience it as appearing before a tribunal where intimate matters are laid bare and where a man should fear judgement. Now, of its very nature, reflection on man's weakness and guilt carries with it an element of pain. But this is only one—and certainly the least important—aspect of the sacramental event. Taken as a whole, the liturgical forgiveness of sins can be experienced as beneficial and grace-bestowing, much more than has up till now been the case.

We have already indicated the need for personal pastoral care in private confession. In addition to this we should like to advocate that the service of penance be understood above all as the event in which we are accepted with all the pettiness that clings to us. The words spoken and sung must express the love and bounty of Jesus as the ultimate and decisive message concerning our lives. Everyone present must be able to hear that 'there is nothing . . . in the world as it is or the world as it shall be . . . that can separate us from the love of God in Christ Jesus our Lord!'[1] In this gathering it must be made clear in the name of the community of human beings and in the name of God that we are accepted just as we are, and that we must accept one another in this way. Hearing and saying this is really grace-giving. 'If that happens to us, we experience grace. After such an experience we may

[1] J. A. T. Robinson, *Honest to God*, SCM Press, London (1963), 128.

not be better than before, and we may not believe more than before. But everything is transformed. In that moment, grace conquers sin and reconciliation bridges the gulf of estrangement. . . . We experience the grace of being able to accept the life of another, even if it be hostile and harmful to us, for, through grace, we know that it belongs to the same Ground to which we belong, and by which we have been accepted.'[1]

It may be asked whether what we are suggesting is realistic and capable of human experience, whether it can be 'announced' by a priest. We acknowledge that success cannot be guaranteed on every occasion, and that if success is to be possible lack of enthusiasm and shyness must be taken into account. The person who comes to a celebration and in the reflection there taking place becomes aware of isolation, weakness and lack of direction is open to the experience of grace. He looks forward to his recognition of guilt being taken up in the proclamation of forgiveness, solidarity and a new mission.

Man wishes for strength and confidence through which, perhaps in spite of a great deal that has occurred, he will once more be able to take up his task with greater zeal. In the administering of private confession it is above all kindness and discretion that are to be demanded of the priest: 'He must be able to accept the penitent in the spirit of Christ and make his own that firm compassion of the Saviour. . . . One is always meeting people who have received rough treatment in the confes-

[1] P. Tillich, *Die letzten Dinge* (1933[4]), 183; quoted by Robinson, 81.

sional. This usually means disaster.'[1] In the service of penance, where no personal confession takes place, the emphasis must be laid on mutual acceptance, on forgiving again and again, on faith in one another. As we have already mentioned, the Christian needs to receive help in order to become conscious of his own bourgeois outlook, false sense of scandal and moral blindness.

The form of liturgical forgiveness of sin

In principle we can distinguish two basic forms of liturgical forgiveness of sins: the communal celebration and private ministration. In actual fact we are only familiar with private confession and the common confession of guilt of the *Confiteor* in the introductory prayers of the mass. This latter, however, is hardly experienced as a real proclamation of grace. Only for a short while have communal celebrations been taking place.

Our own personal opinion is that the introduction of services of penance[2] can hold a great advantage. The second Vatican Council's *Pastoral Constitution on the Sacred Liturgy* expressly states: Whenever rites, according to their specific nature, make provision for communal celebration involving the presence and active participation of the faithful, this way of celebrating them is to be preferred, as far as

[1] A. Snoeck, *Biecht en pastoraal-psychologie*, Bruges (1958), 16 and 42.
[2] The author states that he uses the term *boeteviering* (service of penance) and intentionally avoids the term *biecht-celebratie*, which we translate as 'confessional service', because this term suggests private confession. (Translator.)

possible, to a celebration that is individual and quasi-private.[1]

Dr W. Bekkers, the late bishop of 's-Hertogen-bosch, said about this: 'I should like to describe this celebration as an ecclesiastical rite, whose aim is to make the faithful aware of their guilty relationship to God precisely in solidarity with each other; also to make them aware that God is a seeking God who offers his forgiving mercy especially when the people of God approach him united in repentance, and, finally, to make them aware of the question as to whether now is perhaps the moment for an encounter with God in a personal confession, in which one knows oneself to be aided and supported by the unity of the whole community present.'[2]

The placing of communal celebration in the fore-ground will make possible a clearer perception of the social character of the sacrament, which, after all, should always be a celebration and sign of mutual reconciliation among people. Where this sacrament is experienced as a private affair between God and one individual human being, there is a weakening at work which will also make itself felt outside just as soon as the person discovers that every meaning in life, even the religious, can only be grasped in function of human fellowship. From what we have said about the secularisation of ethics, this will have become clear.

Moreover, the celebration offers great possibilities for the further awareness of social and ecclesial

[1] In *The Documents of Vatican II*, ed. W. M. Abbott S. J. and J. Gallagher, Geoffrey Chapman, London (1966), 148.
[2] W. Bekkers, *Barmhartigheid en biecht*, 15.

dimensions of human sinfulness, as also for a deep formation of conscience through which Christians can be freed from the traditional listing of sins and be brought to an ethic of intention.

We should nevertheless find it a matter for regret were communal celebration to cause private confession to disappear from the faithful's view. Although we do not count ourselves among those who estimate the decline in frequency of confession only as something negative, we are convinced that for the great majority of us, and perhaps for all of us in certain circumstances of life, private confession is most beneficial. Thus we completely agree with Janssen's view: 'We believe that the sacrament of confession in its present form of private confession and absolution has, on scriptural and traditional grounds, a right to exist in the church, today and in the future. Then it may be experienced as a deeply personal human contact, that summons us to complete truthfulness in life, inspired by Christ's radical surrender of his life. We also expect that beside this form of penitential conversion and forgiveness of sins an equal place and sacramental status will be attributed to the forms of communal confession and forgiveness of sins which, in conjunction with an accurate sense of ecclesiastical tradition and gospel, are once more developing.'[1]

To our way of thinking the service of penance and private confession can complete one another in the life of the Christian. Both must be available. We should therefore consider it a great loss if private

[1] G. Janssen, 'Biecht-getuigenis', *Getuigenis* 8 (1964), 346.

confession, as a well-known and easily available institution for everyone, were to fall into neglect. True, there do exist at present a number of undesirable situations in connection with its practice. It is a fact that many have a dislike of it, that they have a feeling of 'getting nowhere' and sometimes of being cross-examined in a painful manner. We do not wish to impose anything on these people. We only wish to keep open the possibility, but in this case a real possibility. And therefore, in the introduction of children to ecclesiastical penance real freedom—and no obligation—will have to be allowed for private confession. Here we would refer to the directives given by Dr P. Moors, Bishop of Roermond, in connection with children's confession and communion. Here, on the grounds of various considerations of pedagogical and theological nature, communal celebration is given priority, but there is also a request for the real possibility of private confession.

We are on the point of attempting to show that the liturgical-sacramental celebration is capable of two forms, or at least can be capable of them. Before we begin, we should like to quote a statement by one of our Protestant brothers, which can perhaps save us from making fatal mistakes: 'We could also bring against the general confession of guilt the objection that it so quickly becomes a dead formula . . . the community "gets bored stiff". In addition to this, if one generally confesses one's guilt together with hundreds of other people, without naming concrete offences, this far more easily becomes a formality than when one personally confesses one's concrete sins before a person holding office in the community or simply before a fellow Christian.'[1]

I should also like to point out that one would be guilty of an oversimplification if one considered the service of penance as the perfect means of escape from the discontent with confession or as the ideal mode of expression of the Christian experience of penance. We shall have to wait for the future to show us whether celebrations in Holland and else-where—where at present they are in general still completely unknown—will also be able to retain their power of attraction over a long period. Prediction concerning the further development of religious sensibility is a precarious undertaking, even though we might take into account our conviction that the man of the future will feel even more strongly than at present an attraction towards communal experiences and expression. But there will always remain the need for quiet and personal self-expression, for understanding, guidance and loving forgiveness directed to the individual person. Spite and enmity will only be able gradually to disappear when theological reflection, preaching and also concrete practice are all directed as much at the communal form as at private administering and experience.

In search of a form for the service of penance

Services of penance are still very much in the experimental stage. There is probably no-one

[1] M. Arntzen, *Biecht en vergeving van zonden*, Kampen (1961), 34.

among us who would think himself capable of giving satisfactory answers to all the questions which could be raised concerning the form and significance of these celebrations. There is need in the first place for real reflection and for practical tests of ideas put forward. In this way we shall all be striving towards a truly beneficial experiencing and ministration of the sacrament.

We shall develop our point of view in confrontation with Dr Bekkers' position:

The community-character does not, however, imply that everything should or even must necessarily take place in a massively collective way. Just the opposite. Community precisely distinguishes itself from the anonymity of the crowd by its call upon the participation of the person as a person. For this reason alone the community-character of the confessional service clearly and expressly implies that within this celebration there is a place for personal, 'secret' confession by the penitent to a confessor. This individual confession is an essential requirement for grave sins. It is most desirable and should be encouraged—without being exhaustive—for all other sins. Also, absolution ought to be given separately, in conjunction with each individual confession. . . . For the faithful who do not wish to proceed to an individual confession within the confessional service, there must be a general, collective acknowledgement of guilt. This will be followed by a prayer for the forgiveness of all. This celebration, however valuable it may be, cannot constitute a sacrament for those who do not individually confess their sins and likewise receive absolution.[1]

The service of penance will usually take place in the evening and at more or less fixed times of the year—for example, during Advent, Lent, and perhaps late summer. With the coming reforms in the liturgy it will probably become possible to hold a service of penance immediately before the eucharistic liturgy just once. As an extension and revaluation of the confession of guilt formerly constituted by the *Confiteor* this would seem an attractive idea. It will certainly appeal to a large number of the faithful. At the moment we are a little shy of putting this into practice. The question is whether through being coupled with the eucharist the service of penance might be neglected and become a somewhat hasty and superficial event in which a general confession of guilt and proclamation of grace takes place, but in which there is no quiet reflection and no real repentance. Furthermore, it seems advisable to hold collective celebrations only a few times during the year and specifically to invite the faithful to them. The success which these celebrations have at the time must not be allowed by priests to deceive them into striving after a high frequency and massive attendance. The first experiments in this field indicate that a rather small number of faithful is best and that it is a good idea to use a small chapel where available. It can therefore be a good thing to hold two celebrations in the afternoon or evening. Then there are less people present, which contributes towards a quietly reflected repentance. The

[1] Bekkers, 16.

chance of personal involvement is undoubtedly greater with those who have come to the church especially for this purpose than with those who 'happen to find themselves' in a service of penance one Sunday.

In convents, where there exists the custom of more or less weekly confession, a communal celebration can certainly be held more often. It is obvious to our way of thinking that religious should take part in parochial celebrations. From the fact that a separate service for nuns is included in this publication it must not be concluded that we are an advocate of separate celebration.

At least until a short while ago confessional services were held in many parishes. As the name clearly suggests, here confession and absolution took place individually and only preparation and thanksgiving were made in common. This is clearly a form of private confession. I am far from being a supporter of these confessional services. Seeing that we consider private administering and communal experiencing as two distinct and mutually referring forms of ecclesiastical-liturgical penance, I object to the two forms being thrust into each other. Nevertheless, I recognise that from a practical point of view the confessional service is often in its rightful place, which is that of being a bridge to completely communal celebration. In such a service it is required that the number of faithful be relatively small in proportion to the priests present, so that a calm, personal confession can really take place within the framework of the service. From my experience it appears that this is quite feasible in a convent which is not too large. However, I doubt whether it could take place in normal parish celebrations, which are open to everyone. Is it not already becoming clear that these services are getting too long and that people become bored because they have to wait so long for their fellow penitents to complete their individual confessions? Some priests advise the faithful to keep their confession as short as possible. Thus many will limit themselves to the very brief rendering of a few facts or choose an expression such as 'I accuse myself of my sinfulness, especially against love and justice.' Hereupon the priest pronounces absolution. An enthusiastic advocate of this practice once told us that he had administered confession to forty Christians in twenty minutes! Now I accept that such haste (in spite of which the celebration seems long-drawn-out) is exceptional. Nevertheless, there is a danger which is not in the least imaginary that, in spite of good intentions, confession will become (or remain) a mechanical and automatic event if the personal contact between confessor and penitent must be achieved within the period of one minute. What can be the value of such a shrivelled-up confession? It cannot be called a self-expression, which enables the priest to make a fair 'judgement'. What else is the priest, then, than an 'absolution automaton', enabling people to get in and out of the confessional more quickly? It is also without doubt possible to formulate the invitation to personal confession in such a way that only a relatively small number make use of it. Care must be taken not to give the impression that only 'great sinners' and 'exceptionally sensitive believers' are eligible for entry into the confessional.

We wish to plead for a service of penance which, in contrast to the confessional service, is characterised by a communal confession of guilt and proclamation of forgiveness, and in which room is left for quiet reflection: a few minutes of consideration and personal prayer, during which time suitable music may be played. After this the celebrant will pronounce a general prayer for mercy and forgiveness over the faithful. At the same time an *invitation* should be made, an invitation to arrive at a personal, private confession during the succeeding days or weeks. In the next section we shall consider this point in more detail.

It must be asked whether in the type of service of penance which we have recommended one can speak of a sacramental event. I am convinced that in this celebration there is mercy and forgiveness for the person who sincerely strives after repentance. The priest, as holder of an office in the church, may also expressly announce this to him. The question of sacramentality will certainly be capable of raising discussion. If one adheres to the requirements which are made by current textbooks for the validity of the sacrament, the answer must be in the negative. Not only is explicit and personal confession lacking, but, moreover, the clearly defined formula of absolution is not used. A present-day problem is not solved, however, simply, by referring to a traditional answer.

Perhaps it is in general worth while reflecting whether the answer to the question concerning the sacramentality of one or other event is always as evident as we so often tend to suppose. Is it, to take another example, really clear that there can still be talk of a sacramental marriage where man and wife are completely alienated from each other and where there is no anthropological reality present forming the basis of this 'marriage made in heaven'? Would there not be sense in asking ourselves about the sacramentality possibly present in the relationship of two unmarried people living together in sincere marital intention and trying to give a Christian form to their lives and those of their children?

If we search for the actual sacramental essence of penance, we shall discover it in the *manifestation* of personal sinfulness before the community of the faithful or possibly before the qualified representative of that community. Upon realising that he has done wrong, been unfaithful and therefore is in need of forgiveness, a person comes before the church, acknowledges his guilt, arrives at a self-expression suited to his personal situation, and asks for forgiveness. Private confession is, from this point of view, really only one particular form of liturgical-sacramental penance. It must not simply stand in the way of the rise of other forms. There are a number of situations in which private confession is truly desirable; the experiencing of a deep and life-gripping personal guilt, the need for personal guidance, the application to growing trust in one's own calling, to mention a few. There are also a number of situations in which communal celebration is more in place, such as the deepening and broadening of our understanding of conscience, the further development of awareness of the social and ecclesial dimension of human sinfulness. With the voice of her teaching authority the church could recognise the communal celebration as sacramental in the strict sense.

We believe that one is guilty of an unjustified generalisation of one's own experience and sometimes even of formalism when one deduces, *a priori*, that the communal confession of guilt such as it takes place in practice is generally of less value than individual confession. For certain people with a tendency towards reflection this will be true: they can experience personal self-expression more deeply. This will also be valid for the person who has arrived at a discovery of his guilt. But in our estimation there are many who come to a more basic confession in communal expression than they do in individual expression. Similarly, we also object to the unfounded generalisation that human activity finds its best form of expression in private confession.

Naturally, one can appeal to currently existing ecclesiastical definitions. These constitute the reason why we have avoided any strict formula of absolution in the services offered here. But the person who relies purely on definitions for the defence of his position is the person who has to wait for permission to change his opinion.

Isn't an explicit confession before a priest required for 'mortal sins'? This question loses its cogent character as soon as one accepts the interpretation of gradation in sin suggested by us and the remarks we made on the secularisation of ethics. We are acquainted with the Council of Trent's statement that all mortal sins committed after baptism and not yet directly forgiven by the power entrusted to the church must be confessed, together with their number, their nature and those circumstances which affect the nature of sins.[1] We

[1] Denzinger-Schönmetzer, 1707.

also know that the early church thought somewhat differently in this matter. Not only was a precise definition in confessional matters foreign to her, but she also knew many variations with regard to offences which were required to be subject to ecclesiastical penance. Perhaps we may say that for its time, and within the atmosphere of the thought of its day, Trent expressed in a sharp and even somewhat over-precise formulation its inward conviction that the man who is conscious of having committed a serious offence needs to realise clearly that he may not simply carry on as usual. He must be aware that he has wounded the body of the church and that he is slowing down her development. He must recognise that he therefore stands in need of forgiveness from his neighbour, from the community—i.e., the ecclesial community—and from God. Thus a personal confession before the church is certainly in place, and must be considered the most obvious way of asking for reconciliation and renewed participation in the life of the community; for this reason the priest will invite the Christian to do precisely this.

For the future we should not like to see this confession before the church prescribed by a definite law, but to leave the Christian free to choose it for himself; also, the 'confession before the church' should not be simply reduced to confession before an appointed priest. This desire for confession can be encouraged and even aroused by priestly preaching.

But, it may be said, sacraments are holy signs. Their administering is an official ecclesiastical deed. Thus they may only be administered to those who are found worthy of them. Is it not for the priest, as the holder of an office, to judge a person's suitability? How can he exercise this *krisis* if he does not personally meet the individual in the confession of sins?

In order to preclude misunderstanding, let me at once expressly and fundamentally recognise the meaningfulness of ecclesiastical discipline. It is already clear from the New Testament writings that Christians were, on the grounds of their unworthy public behaviour, excluded by the local apostle or presbyter from participation in the eucharistic celebration. The church must take constant action against sin within her midst. The question which we find ourselves facing is: should the actual decisive judgement on whether the Christian is worthy to take part in the celebration of the eucharist usually be made by the priest or by the person himself? Apart from cases where the ecclesiastical disciplinary judgement is directed against the public offender and where we have to do with 'binding and loosing' in the biblical sense,[1] the Christian himself is fundamentally responsible. Here we may make reference to Augustine:

> The Christian, who after baptism has sinned gravely, must externalise this self-accusation. 'Confession' to God must be made concrete by some external and severe penance. What has been admitted to God must be publicly acknowledged by expiation. Self-accusation of grave sin must first be expressed by voluntary abstention from the eucharist, because the Christian has become unworthy of participation in the sacrifice of the

[1] Karl Rahner, 'Forgotten Truths concerning the Sacrament of Penance' in *Theological Investigations*, vol. II.

community. This 'liturgical excommunication' corresponds to the sinner's real position and expresses his self-condemnation, the condition for pardon.[1]

It is for the priest to further this self-judgement of the Christian by giving advice, when asked, by inspiring truly personal conscience, and by faithful preaching of the gospel of Jesus Christ. His preaching will still have to be directed towards adult humanity and Christianity in even stronger terms than today. The emphasis must be laid on the cultivation of a personal Christianity lived with conviction. We must offer support to one another, not least when it is a question of discovering the content of our life's mission. A truly mature conscience can only be the ever newly acquired possession of the person who is prepared to listen. It is a great illusion to imagine that we might just purely and simply, without continual effort, have that purity of ambition and clearness of insight which enable us, in the various situations of life, to see sufficiently clearly the concrete implications of our responsibility towards ourself and towards the person with whom we are called to live in community. Our conscience is formed in a continual dialogue, in persistent co-operation with God, who speaks to us in many ways: in our silent reflection and prayer, in our listening to Christ, the Word of the Father, as he speaks to us in the witness of scripture and the preaching of the church, in our neighbour, as he is together with us in person and

[1] Thus does Paul Anciaux give Augustine's view in *The Sacrament of Penance*, Challoner Publications, Tenbury Wells (1962), 49–50.

community. But we cannot do more than direct ourselves towards the word, the expectation, and the example of the other person. And this is true even when we know that a particular fellow human being is officially called to speak to us. The most he can do is to outline very carefully boundaries to our mission and responsibility. Perhaps he may be able to indicate a particular domain to us, perhaps tell us that a particular choice is not truly in accord with sound humanity, perhaps guide our growth towards maturity and express his expectations of us. But ultimately he cannot have the last word that expresses the immediate content of our task. No-one may ask another a question which he himself is alone capable of answering.

The place of private confession in the life of the Christian

We have already spoken several times about the significance of private confession. We shall not repeat here what has been said before. On the whole, private confession arises from the invitation of the priest and the desire of the Christian. The priest's invitation must be quite unrestricted, with respect to place as well as to time. Having described the church and confessional as the most obvious place for the present, Dr Bekkers wrote:

In addition to this, however, someone who seriously asks for the sacrament of confession must be able to confess anywhere: in a confessional room, in a parlour, on a home visit, in a railway carriage, and so on. Thus we need adaptability that is as supple as possible. For many the confessional will remain a protective little corner, but many have an understandable dislike of this place.[1]

It would be a good thing if churches were to be equipped with a confessional room, so that the faithful might be able to choose between an open conversation there, and the semi-dark, whispered contact of the confessional. A person will quite often come to the recognition of guilt and the request for express ecclesiastical forgiveness on the occasion of a home visit. At such a time the administering of private confession is in its proper place. The priest will try to pray together with the Christian and in this prayer will pronounce forgiveness over him. It is quite possible that under some circumstances this forgiveness might be pronounced, for example, over man and wife together.

> The same is true of times of confession. Saturday afternoon seems to have become completely unsuitable as the only time of confession. Perhaps Saturday morning offers better opportunities, but there should, in addition to this, always exist the possibility of confession for those who seriously request it. In this matter priests must be as much as possible at the service of other people.[2]

It is only during liturgical services, the eucharistic celebration, for example, that there must be no opportunity for confession. We would rather not have any administering of private confession in connection with services of penance. We recognise that the one form of penance can call up the other,

[1] Bekkers, 14. [2] Bekkers, 14.

but this does not mean that we must actually join them together—for example, by following a fully communal service of penance with private confession.

The Christian's desire for private confession can arise from various origins, as I have explained at length in the first chapter. Such a desire will often be sincerely expressed by the person who desires a personal conversation and spiritual guidance. At least at the great moments of life, when a man experiences his calling more clearly, when he is conscious of taking a new task upon himself or of laying aside an old one, he will wish for the deeply personal proclamation of God's mercy and good pleasure. When repentance grasps us more sharply and deeply, above all in the awareness of having seriously fallen short, many of us will do well to confess our sins in private confession.

Personally, I estimate this confession before a priest very highly, since it is a sincere and undisguised self-expression of the human being who recognises how much he has made the still continuing disruption of the world also his own. For this reason the confession must also be concrete: to be confessed are those events which oppress the person at that moment and which he considers serious. Furthermore, I consider that every adult should reflect upon his fundamental attitude and actual plan of life regularly indulging in an 'examination of conscience',[1] in which he should try to trace

[1] I have enclosed this term in inverted commas intentionally because I know that it is all too often taken to mean an unhealthy sifting and rooting out of a person's mind. Suggestions for an authentic examination of conscience are to be found in R. Guardini, *Das Gute, das Gewissen und die Sammlung*, Mainz (1953), and in E. Fromm, *The Art of Loving*, London (1957).

the background and motives of his actions. It is obvious that the object of this reflection will be constituted by the various spheres of life which the person in question enters. It would seem advisable to include at least the conclusions of such a searching of conscience in one's confession.

For most people a straightforward confessing of their concrete sins is advisable. Bonhoeffer made several very true remarks concerning this matter some years ago.[1] Do we not often deceive ourselves somewhat with our so-called acknowledgement before God in the silence and seclusion of our heart:

> We must ask ourselves whether we have not often been deceiving ourselves with our confession of sin to God, whether we have not rather been confessing our sins to ourselves and also granting ourselves absolution. And is not the reason perhaps for our countless relapses and the feebleness of our Christian obedience to be found precisely in the fact that we are living on self-forgiveness? Self-forgiveness can never lead to a break with sin; this can be accomplished only by the judging and pardoning Word of God itself.
>
> Who can give us the certainty that, in the confession and the forgiveness of our sins, we are not dealing with ourselves but with the living God? God gives us this certainty through our brother. Our brother breaks the circle of self-deception.[2]

In my view, Bonhoeffer's statement is a true one.

[1] D. Bonhoeffer, *Life Together*, SCM Press, London (1954), 100–12.
[2] Bonhoeffer, *Life Together*, 105–6.

We are all exposed to the temptation of self-deception. In our daily life quite often there is a need to keep at least some faults hidden. Inauthenticity and hypocrisy constitute a real threat. Sincere confession to another person can free us from them. When he really becomes our brother and engages himself in our situation another person can help us with our confused conscience and speak to us words of encouragement or of admonition. In the expression, and thereby the testing of our conscience by the insight of another, we can situate the evil in our life. We mature through this recognition and arrive at a new beginning: 'When a person does not arrive at precisely situating and expressing in a clear confession the evil that he carries within him, then the urge to remain consistent with the attitude acquired has the upper hand.'[1]

The priest's answer to a real self-expression should not be merely a pious platitude and the giving of a meaningless penance of a few Hail Marys. Rahner acknowledges that in this aspect of private confession we have a situation which cannot be changed overnight. 'But should one see this situation, one would understand that the person who sees no problems about it must have a juridical, formalistic idea of sin or must think of the sacrament in a magico-mechanical way.'[2]

The first penance that every person must take upon himself consists in trying to accept his situation in a positive way, knowing that the suffering and pain which he will meet with are always the joint

[1] Snoeck, *Biecht en psychoanalyse*, Bruges (1957), 24.
[2] K. Rahner, 'Beichtprobleme' in *Theological Investigations*, vol. III.

consequence of his own sin and that of other people. Because we live so little for the other person, his existence constantly remains dark and solitary. With this conviction the priest may pronounce the final prayer 'May the Passion of Our Lord Jesus Christ . . .'. Doubtless, in most cases a penance consisting of prayer will rightly be chosen, especially with the more frequent devotional confession. But it is a question whether a penance can actually be imposed. Should the situation not rather be that the priest stands by the penitent's side, aiding him in his attempt to see where there are real possibilities of restoring what he has damaged and what he can do in order to make his life more deeply inspired by love? In saying this I am not seeking the path of least resistance, but attempting really to bring penance into conversion, to make it into a very palpable and real expression of the renewed choice for the attitude of faith and love in the everyday routine of life.

Here I shall bring our reflections to a close. I started off from the deadlock in traditional confessional practice, to conclude with a word on penance. As I close my study I am more conscious than when I commenced that I have been considering a difficult problem. 'Guilt is not objective in the sense of something which is outside or above a person. Guilt leads its existence within the intensely personal bond between man and truth. . . . Is not the greatest task of man, today as much as ever before, that of growing, in spite of everything that threatens to alienate him from himself, to real humanity?'[1]

[1] 'Op verzoek', *Ruimte*, 3, 3–4.

Part 2

Services of
Penance for Adults

Edited by P. J. Mars and F. J. Heggen

Comments on the Services

1. It is advisable not to adopt the services offered here too hastily. The celebrant or organising team, whichever is the case, must have obtained a clear idea beforehand of the meaning and value of such services. We would therefore advise beginning cautiously. In the first place, the priest needs to become well acquainted with the theological background. Study and perhaps group discussion must first take place.

The faithful can be prepared and instructed through preaching and group discussion. We are of the opinion that at least three or four sermons are necessary in order to explain the central idea of the conversion to which Jesus Christ summons us.

2. The services are not necessarily to be used just as they are given here. They are only intended as an example and a stimulus. According to individual preference one or another may be omitted or combined. The main thing is that anyone who uses these or other services should make *careful, written*

preparation and make sure that he preserves a clear plan and an explicit theme. It is a good thing to distribute a programme of the service among the faithful so that they may more clearly perceive the central idea, and may achieve a more complete personal contact in communal prayer. This programme is best composed by the parish priest, taking into account the nature of his parish. For this reason we have refrained from composing any sort of booklet for the faithful.

3. Both in the preceding theoretical exposition and in the Services which follow we have addressed ourselves to adults.

4. It is of prime importance that the fact that a 'celebration of salvation' is here taking place should be shown to full advantage. These services bring us together as a community of human beings who are weighed down by sinfulness, insufficiency and alienation from each other. We are searching for wholeness, for a future, for salvation. We believe that this is offered to us in Jesus Christ. He unites us around himself. He proclaims to us hope and faith in forgiveness and liberation. He summons us to repentance, to the recognition of our guilt and the repairing of what we have so greatly destroyed. He shows us how we must penetrate through the external deed into our heart, to the attitude which inspires our outward behaviour and ultimately determines our morality. Following the example of Christ we can endure and forgive, but are also established anew in our calling and are made capable of realising new possibilities.

With the help of holy scripture this event of salvation needs to be made evident in the service of penance. In the various services the accent will be laid on different aspects.

5. We must not fall once again into narrowness in the practice of penance, as has all too often happened in the past. Partly for this reason, we are critical of services in which, during the celebration itself, large numbers are invited to individual confession in a confessional or confessional room. We very much doubt whether these evening services, in which the faithful prepare themselves together for separately administered confession, have any real future. The danger which threatens is that the sacrament of penance will be experienced in just as impersonal and formalistic a manner as before. Whilst it is a strong possibility that some Christians may wish to go on from the communal celebration to a personal self-expression before the priest in private confession, and that in such cases the celebration is *in fact* playing a preparatory role, the most obvious arrangement seems to be that of a certain variation between communal and individual celebrations. A private confession occurring in conjunction with communal celebration will thus be the exception; hence, it may profit one person more, according to the structure of his personality and the total situation in which he exists, to take part in a communal celebration, whilst another may do better to place the accent on private confession.

6. It does not seem to us to be a good idea to attempt to give to the faithful gathered for the celebration an account of the theological merits of such services, their sacramentality, their validity with regard to absolution, etc. We must not confuse them, but, on the basis of our own personally matured and well-

considered view, simply let them experience the beneficial character of the service, proclaiming with emphasis the forgiveness of sins for everyone who engages himself sincerely.

7. As far as possible, one should have different people coming forward in the services for proclamations and preaching, the confession of guilt and the litanies, the prayers and the readings from scripture. This means that priests who are ministering in one parish only will do well to hold these services together with colleagues from other parishes. A mutual exchange of ideas, a change of pulpit, preparation by a team, seem advisable from all points of view. Doubtless, one may also have the reading done by lay people, who will come forward from among those present.

8. In the services of penance which we have designed, a space of a few minutes is left for personal reflection. We believe that it is a good thing to play music during this period.

As general rules we propose: (a) no vocal music. This distracts because attention is paid to the text; (b) no solo concertos or instrumental solo pieces. By their virtuoso character and their individuality they attract fascinated attention.

The most suitable music seems to be: (a) concerti grossi from the late baroque period: Corelli, Handel, Vivaldi and others; (b) symphonies from the early classical period: Mozart, Haydn; in other words, objective—as it were, 'absolute'—music with a joyful character. The music should not be obtrusively loud.

9. The choice of material for singing by the community present will depend on the possibilities in

each particular place. For this reason one must make one's choice. Even with a comparatively difficult group of people it is possible to practise the refrain of an appropriate psalm, and this takes no more than a few minutes. A choir or a handful of singers can sing the verses. Care should be taken not to choose only penitential and supplicatory psalms and hymns.

10. In this English translation, Grail-Gelineau psalms and hymns have, for the sake of convenience, been cited from one source: *Praise the Lord*, Geoffrey Chapman, London (1966), though other psalms and hymns from different sources may of course be used instead. Biblical quotations are throughout taken from the new *Jerusalem Bible*, and it is strongly recommended that this version should be used for the bible readings.

First general service

theme: our attitude towards sin

1. Opening part

Organ music is played during the entry of the celebrant and his assistants.

Blessing: May he who helps us when we refuse to give up, help you all to be tolerant with each other, following the example of Christ Jesus, so that united in mind and voice you may give glory to the God and Father of our Lord Jesus Christ. (Rom 15: 5–6.)

Let us sing, praying for God's mercy and kindness (*or, where applicable:* Let us join in the prayer of the choir . . .): *the hymn* 'Love divine, all Loves excelling' (*Praise the Lord,* 129).

2. Service of the Word

Brothers and sisters, we human beings are for ever coming into conflict with each other through our faults and shortcomings. Clear evidence of this fact is provided by the large number of words we have to describe the ways in which we can react: we can be obstinate or hard-hearted, for instance; we can sulk, hate, argue, quarrel, complain, make a fuss; we can own up, admit, confess, acknowledge our guilt, ask for forgiveness, make amends, turn over a new leaf. We can talk things over with each other, endure and accept, make allowances and say nothing, forgive and forget. We can also help and support each other, encourage and comfort each other; we can go out to meet other people half way, go along with them; we can open up an entirely new perspective by deciding to go through life with them.

Good and evil live side by side. Weeds grow among the wheat in the heart of every human being. Christ speaks of this in Matthew's gospel.

Reading: Mt 13: 24–30.

Hymn between readings: 'Come, ye thankful people, come' (*Praise the Lord,* 130).

The Lord also speaks to us about our attitude towards evil:

Reading: Lk 6: 27–42.

Homily: Someone once wrote: 'There was once a man who was without fault. He was himself a fault.' Of no one may we require that he be without fault. We ourselves are not so. Others have to suffer through us; they suffer more than we generally realise, because of our character, our whims and peculiarities.

Perhaps we do realise what others have to put up with in us. Perhaps we feel discouraged in our struggle to be without blemish. Perhaps we have not been to confession for quite a time, because when we did we nevertheless still remained the same person.

There is only one human being who is pure,

without sin: Jesus Christ. Scripture shows us his attitude towards the evil in man. 'Love your enemies', he says, 'be merciful; do not condemn, for you cannot see into the other person's heart. Rather acquit, presume goodness.'

We easily respond to hate by hating, through thick and thin we demand our rights, we work out our anger on the other person, or we become obstinately silent towards one another. But Christ did not show us such an example. He behaved in a different way: his actions are liberating and he speaks generosity. He does not condemn a man because he has fallen short. He eats with sinners and proclaims to them forgiveness of their sins, on condition that they are not complacent, but looking, in recognition of their own imperfection, for a hand to support them.

We have a power over those who are guilty towards us in any way. Christ does not use that power; he acquits.

The person who hates and bears malice is trying to bring the other person under his power, to subject him to his own wishes. Christ says: 'Father, forgive them; for they know not what they do.' Hate becomes powerless. Love liberates, love disarms and makes possible the return of the other person to us.

Jesus Christ accepts human beings with their weakness. He invites, he looks into a person's heart, sees his attempt, often so hidden, to be good and warmhearted.

We must walk in his footsteps, not judging and condemning, but accepting and forgiving. 'Do as you would be done by', as the proverb so rightly tells us: every person has a right to room in which to be himself, has a right to understanding and may ask for forgiveness. This is true of each of us. We must accept ourself; also, with our lack of perfection, we must become reconciled with ourself. We also can and may live a life of freedom.

Our intention in celebrating this service of penance is to find the truly authentic Christian attitude towards evil in ourselves and in others. We have come together to express our repentance, to make good and, in the spirit and strength of the Lord, to relieve one another of guilt. Jesus teaches us to pray at such a time as this: Forgive us our debts, as we have forgiven those who are in debt to us. In Matthew's gospel he adds these words to the Our Father:

> If you forgive others their failings, your heavenly Father will forgive you yours; but if you do not forgive others, your Father will not forgive your failings either. (Mt 6: 14–15.)

This penance is a free gift of God, but at the same time it is also a task for us—a call to us to make reparation, to forgive generously and willingly.

3. Reflection on our lives

Before we reflect on our lives, let us pray to Christ, who became the Lamb of God for us:

Let us ask ourselves:

Whether we hate, avoid, and refuse to speak to certain people, because they once rebuffed us; whether we have caused them suffering.
Do we really want to forgive and forget?
Do we at least want to try to forgive and forget by

doing nothing hostile towards them again?
Do we want to endure patiently and keep silent?
Do we dare to acknowledge our own faults?
Do we make amends, for example, when we have spoken evil of others?
Do we take up a wait-and-see attitude after a quarrel, or can we be the first to try and repair the relationship?
Do we believe in the forgiveness of sins?
Are we despondent, because we were seeking perfection rather than forgiveness?
Our calling is to promote in our own situation Christ's spirit of willingness to forgive, of reconciliation and forbearance.
Are we conscious of this?
Do we really try to work for this?
Do we pray to have the spirit of Jesus?

Pause during which music is played.

4. Confession of guilt and prayer for forgiveness

I confess to almighty God
and to all who are present here,
that I have sinned,
that I have fallen short.
Of all those to whom I have caused any sort of pain,
of all those to whom I have caused offence,
I ask forgiveness.
Lord, be merciful to me, a sinner.

Celebrant: The Lord will be merciful to you and will forgive you your sins. May he shelter you from evil and guard you against temptation. May everyone forgive you and no longer remember your faults.

5. Prayer for those who suffer under our sins

Celebrant: Lord, hear us.

Community of the faithful: Lord, graciously hear us.

Celebrant: Bless those who are hostile towards us and let us become reconciled with one another. Lord, hear us.

Community: Lord, graciously hear us (*repeated after each petition*).

Celebrant: We pray to you for those whom we have wronged: grant them health and salvation.

May those to whom we have brought suffering meet with affection.

Stand by those who are disillusioned, that they may be able to believe in a future.

Give support to lonely wives and husbands and to disappointed parents: may their loved ones return to them.

Comfort the innocent who are under suspicion and make them free through truth.

Enlighten those who have to pass judgement on the guilty: may their judgements be wise and just.

We pray above all for those who, through our own shortcomings and the shortcomings of the society in which we live, have become confused and bewildered and have followed the wrong paths.

Come, O Holy Spirit, enlighten the hearts of all who look to your aid, and kindle in them the fire of your love.

Send forth your Spirit, that all may be created afresh and the earth renewed.

Let us pray: O God, you have taught the hearts of your faithful through the enlightenment of your Holy Spirit; grant that by the same Spirit we may possess true wisdom and always rejoice in his consolation. This we ask of you through Jesus Christ, your Son, our Lord. Amen.

6. Final chant

Psalm 99 (100): 'Cry out with joy to the Lord, all the earth' (*Praise the Lord*, 165); *or hymn* 'All people that on earth do dwell' (*Praise the Lord*, 138).

Second general service

theme: the forward-looking community

1. Opening part

The priest asks for forgiveness: Lord, I am a sinful human being, and I ask for your forgiveness. Make me worthy to be your servant and to represent the people gathered here.

(*The priest could at this point put on his stole and surplice.*)

Opening prayer for the community: May the almighty and merciful Lord grant us remission of all our sins.

2. Service of the Word

We have come together on account of our guilt and sinfulness. From one another and from God we seek liberation and unburdening; we wish to confess our guilt and to ask for forgiveness. We believe that this will do us good, that we shall go away from here as different people. Such is our faith, such is the experience of the people of God. Let us listen to this in the letter of the apostle John and in a psalm of the people of Israel.

Reading: 1 Jn 1: 8–2: 2.

Psalm between readings: Psalm 102 (103) 'My soul, give thanks to the Lord' (*Praise the Lord*, 166).

The fact that, although people have been doing penance for centuries, sin has not been driven from the world, might tend to discourage us. We might be tempted to think that, after all, everything stays the same, that the world does not improve. The apostle John thought otherwise, and described for us in poetic form his expectation of the final outcome. This is his vision of a new earth, which will at the same time be heaven, the New Jerusalem, where God will dwell among his creatures.

Reading: Rev 21: 1–5.

Suggestion for the homily: Pope John wrote the encyclicals *Mater et Magistra* and *Pacem in Terris*. In them he spoke about the United Nations and other world organisations, about co-operation at world level, about aid to developing countries, about social rights and pensions for old people, widows, and invalids, about each person's responsibility in his own occupation, about participation in science, culture, and technology.

Some people find it strange that a pope should speak about these subjects: 'An encyclical ought not to concern itself with such worldly matters.' The person who talks in this way sees the world as a lost vale of tears, without real meaning for the Christian, only to be considered as a practising ground for Christian perfection.

In reality it is man's task to bring the world to full development, to build up a community of peace, of prosperity for everyone, of deep humanity. In the development which the world is going through we can point to two mutually connected phenomena: progress in the technical, economic, and scientific fields, and the ever-closer weaving together of the lives of individuals and peoples. It is becoming less and less possible to live 'separately' from others and from each other. This demands reflection. We must recognise these phenomena in their true light, so that technical and economic progress may indeed further humanity. Here are some examples.

Through modern means of transport, anyone can suddenly have enormous powers at his disposal. He has therefore much greater responsibility for the life of his fellow men.

The presence of television in the home demands selection of programmes on the basis of joint consideration.

Portable radios are often stumbling blocks. The telephone enables us to deprive others of their rest and freedom.

Modern techniques make it possible for us to influence others. The education of children has for quite some time rested no longer with parents, school and immediate environment, but has become an affair of the whole community, which by its means of communication—books, radio, films, television—reaches everyone and thus influences everyone.

Modern business undertaking demands co-operation, teamwork, mutual adaptation, understanding of the difficulties of adaptation for old people and newcomers; it tempts many into shifting responsibility on to others.

The nursing of the sick and the elderly is mostly

carried out in an excellent way in specialised institutions. But these sick and elderly people are out of our sight and very often from our hearts.

The increasing population demands greater housing and flat building, but at the same time brings loneliness for many and the very real threat of impersonal administration.

Contact between people living throughout the world is becoming easier and easier. We can come into one another's presence more easily. Are we truly closer to each other?

All this requires a Christian examination and a pure, unprejudiced approach. Hitherto unsuspected perspectives of a new earth are opening up. Man is lord of the world, creation is entrusted to him, so that he may employ it in his own salvation and bring it to greater perfection.

This all demands reflection, it demands the gathering together of communities such as this one. In the communal service of penance we are searching for the spirit of Jesus Christ in order to be able to live together facing the future. It is not our main intention to study closely all the faults of which we are guilty, but to experience this celebration as a summons to reflection, toleration and understanding of the tensions experienced by everyone in a crisis of growth such as this.

It is going to become more and more difficult to set up fixed, sharply defined norms of Christian living in this world. The complexity and differentiation of modern life demand a personal approach which must be adapted to any particular situation. Hence the importance of an adult conscience which knows how to consider and consult, but which is capable of an independent judgement. Hence also the necessity of basic attitudes which are Christian, such as: respect for our neighbour, readiness to serve, human solidarity, loyalty to one's word, sincerity towards one another, effort and interest in one's work, honesty in both the spoken and written word.

· We feel ourselves bound up with the whole of humanity. In the strength and example of Jesus Christ let us try to ward off evil and to promote good.

3. Reflection on our lives

Let us reflect on our lives, on our involvement in the process of the world.

Pause, during which music is played.

Now, two of the faithful come forward and alternately lead the community in prayer. The first prayer-leader addresses God in the name of the community present, and prays:

O Lord, the Lord who leads humanity through the centuries, we are confused by the development taking place in our time, we are in danger of wrongly using the possibilities of creation. Atomic weapons, brainwashing, traffic dangers all threaten our humanity. Through what we say or write, we sometimes confuse ourselves and others. We still have to learn how to use radio, newspaper and television in such a way that we do not impudently break into the intimate world of other people out of a lust for sensation, in such a way that we do not mislead public opinion with an unfair representation of events.

Therefore Lord, listen to our prayer.

Both prayer-leaders together: Lord, have mercy upon us.
[*which may be sung to a simple melody*]

All present repeat: Lord, have mercy upon us.

The second leader proceeds:
The development of science and technology, of economy and culture, which you grant us, almighty Lord, needs for that reason to be inspired by the spirit of love.
We confess our guilt in falling short.
Let us recognise our responsibility, so that we may open to everyone the possibility of study and development, and bring prosperity where there is need, medicine and medical care, giving our work for the prosperity and further development of the community.

Both prayer-leaders together: Lord, have mercy upon us.

All present repeat: Lord, have mercy upon us.

The first leader continues:
We are troubled by living together with each other, by lack of accommodation, we are intolerant and blind to the needs of other people; we live in discord with our neighbours and try to outdo them.
Often we are tardy and lazy in carrying out our jobs; in business we allow ourselves to be led by love of money.
We are often unhelpful to our neighbours and members of our family.
The sick, the elderly and those who are alone in life become lonely; we treat one another so often as

numbers and so little as human beings who long for warm-heartedness and sympathy.

Both leaders: Lord, have mercy upon us.

All present: Lord, have mercy upon us.

The second leader continues:
Lord, the environment into which our youth is received is unhealthy, because of its downright adoration of money, because of its unhealthy and unrealistic representation of sex as being purely an instrument of pleasure, because of over-intense competition and jealousy.
Let us take young people into the world of work with special care. We must at least try to understand what is going on inside them and what occupies their interests. We ask you to let us see young people as given by you, as the new generation to whom we can entrust the future.

Both leaders: Lord, have mercy upon us.

All present: Lord, have mercy upon us.

The first leader continues:
There are many areas in the world suffering need, where hunger, sickness and poverty are present on a massive scale; we acknowledge, Lord, that we are too seldom conscious of this, that we, as prosperous people, do not provide generous and unselfish help, that we so hesitatingly join in and regularly support our countrymen who have gone there to devote themselves to the work of building up and of spreading the gospel.

We pray you to release us from the tensions between peoples, from all colonialism, from all discrimination between races and nations. Teach the nations to live together in peace, in brotherly cooperation, in freedom and respect for one another.

Both leaders: Lord, have mercy upon us.

All present: Lord, have mercy upon us.

The second leader continues:
Finally, Lord, we confess, as the church gathered together here, that we are guilty:
We were divided as Christians;
we closed ourselves up in our own traditions, instead of, like you, going forth with willingness to serve and to give our efforts for the well-being of the world.
We lacked the awareness that we could be your people, a sign of salvation and hope for everyone, through our love and our faith.
Therefore we pray you to let a renewing spirit go through your church,
so that each of us may see his task as a Christian in the world of today,
so that we may find support in one another,
so that we may live courageously, trusting in the growth of your kingdom amongst us.

Both leaders: Lord, have mercy upon us.

All present: Lord, have mercy upon us.

4. Proclamation of forgiveness

Celebrant: Listen to Christ's words: Jn 14: 15–21 (*or, alternatively,* Jn 10: 11–16).
Everyone who is of good will is loved by the Lord. His sins are forgiven him. The Spirit of Christ

will be in him. He may go forth from here consoled and strengthened. May the suffering and death of our Lord Jesus Christ, the merits of his holy mother and all holy Christians, all the good you do and all the suffering you bear, bring you remission of your sins, growth in grace, and the reward of everlasting life. Amen.

5. Final psalm of thanksgiving

In conclusion let us sing Psalm 22 (23): 'The Lord is my shepherd' (*Praise the Lord*, 157) (*or* the hymn: 'O praise ye the Lord (*Praise the Lord*, 149)).

Service for religious

theme: availability for the church

1. Opening part

Doxology: How great and wonderful are all your works, Lord God Almighty: just and true are all your ways, King of nations. Who would not revere and praise your name, O Lord? You alone are holy, and all the pagans will come and adore you for the many acts of justice you have shown. (Rev 15: 3–4.) Let us pray to God for mercy: 'Attende Domine' (*Liber usualis*).

2. Service of the Word

Reverend sisters. Let us listen to a passage from Roger Schutz' book, *This Day belongs to God:*

> To love the church as Christ loved her is to accept the fact that the way forward lies over the ruts made by the sin of her children, by their spirit of division and self-sufficiency. It is to love her despite the mediocrity of certain of those of her members who have great responsibilities. It is to love the church in her members, in the finest but also in the weakest of her children.

That is how the church progresses down the ages. The extent of her vitality depends on the extent to which her institutions are animated by the love of her members. She is strong when her members day by day equip themselves with the infinite patience that comes from faith. She is humble when her children, far from making judgements with the bitterness bred of self-satisfaction, agree to love her to the extent of offering their lives to the task of renewing her institutions each and every day. . . .

Our responsibility is to be the leaven in the dough. Of some it is demanded that they should express unity by their words, others have the gift of very fervent intercession, of yet others is asked the offering of their life, the gift of themselves, which may necessitate a bitter struggle, an offering the meaning of which remains hidden.[1]

Reading: 1 Cor 12: 4–31.

Psalm between readings: Psalm 22 (23): 'The Lord is my shepherd' (*Praise the Lord,* 157).

Reading: Mt 10: 1, 5–13.

Suggestion for the homily: Every human being may live his life in the knowledge that he has been called and sent forth by God. This is clear from scripture: God summons each of us to be just the person and also totally the person that only each of us can be, here or anywhere (see Is 43: 1; Jer 1: 4–7; Mk 3: 13; Jn 10: 3; 10: 14–15; Rom 8: 30; 1 Cor 7: 17). He places me on the stage in order to play my role in the drama which has already begun; a role that is

[1] Roger Schutz, *This Day belongs to God,* London (1961), 65–6.

not the same as that of any other person. God has given us each our existence and calls us into the time and space in which our lives are to be lived, by our own name. This is the real name we possess, the real possibility of being ourselves fully. The person who is unfaithful to God is at the same time unfaithful to himself.

We have all been called, we all have the task of building the city of God, which means creating, with faith in the Father of Jesus Christ, goodness and humanity around us. In this much all our vocations are the same. In this much lay people and religious are identical. They know it is their duty to labour at the construction of a kingdom of love and service. There is no difference in calling that cuts as far as the ground of our existence.

Yet there is diversity of gift and function. First and foremost we have a duty unselfishly to acknowledge this diversity, to respect the other person and his talents, really, without jealousy, to give him the freedom to live up to the name he has received from God. We must also have faith in ourselves. Of course, there are a great many things of which others are capable, whilst we are not. But it is certainly just as true that there is something—in fact, very much— of which we are capable whilst others are not. What really matters is that every person should accept himself with his limitations, not being over-anxious to be someone else, but believing himself to be faced with a task with regard to his fellow men and the world.

The passage from Matthew which we have just heard shows how the person who puts himself at the service of the church and of the proclamation of the gospel must live. He is the one who is sent forth, who must at all times be mobile, ready to go: he goes out and away to the unknown, to the new task where the church now has need of him. Availability seems to be an essential element of his life: giving one's effort where it is needed at the present moment and always being ready to go on, from town to town.

He brings peace wherever he comes, he cures the sick, cleanses the lepers, he is the man for others.

The person who gives himself to the church does not try to obtain gold or silver, he does not rely on power, but on the Spirit. He does not exploit people, but stands ready to serve, unceasingly.

3. Reflection on our lives

Let us express our faith in God's calling and sing 'Ad te levavi' (Introit of 1st Sunday of Advent, *Liber usualis*).

Let us ask ourselves:

Do we exalt ourselves above others, above our neighbour in the community, above the Christian in the world?

Are we warm-hearted people who can welcome one another's successes without becoming jealous?

Do we put our faith in the church, in our own calling, in spite of the mediocrity of some and of ourself?

Are we free people, who can change our opinions and know how to listen to others?

Do we dare to admit to fellow members of our community and to others that we are petty, limited and sometimes conceited people?

Do we admit to being wrong and are we true to our word?

Do we perceive need, do we recognise loneliness, and do we go out of our way to help the lonely?

Do we really want to serve the church, so that we gracefully hand over activities which are perhaps dear to us, but can now be carried out by lay people?

Let us pray for the Spirit of Jesus.

Pause during which music is played.

4. Confession of guilt and prayer for forgiveness

I confess to God, the almighty Father,
to Mary, the mother of our faith,
to all the saints and to everyone here present,
that I have fallen and have sinned through slothfulness and selfishness.

I acknowledge that I have been insensitive to the call which God addressed to me in the requests of my neighbour.

Therefore I ask the blessed virgin, Mary, all the saints, you, father, and all those here present to pray to God for me, to be merciful towards me and to support me in goodness.

Lord, grant that we may continually grow towards maturity in faith, trust and love.

All: Hear us, we pray (*repeated after each petition*).

Lord, grant that our lives may more and more resemble that of Jesus Christ.

Lord, grant that our lives for our neighbour may be a visible form of your love.

Lord, grant us a sincere and authentic experience of the goodness of our human existence.

Lord, grant that our lives may be inspired by kindness and patience.

Lord, grant that we may be purified from pride, false pretence and inauthenticity.

Lord, grant that we have an aversion for wrong and find joy in the truth.

The celebrant raises his hands over the faithful and prays:

May the God who saves have mercy upon you. May he show you his loving kindness and remove all your sins.

May the blessing of almighty God, of the Father, Son, and Holy Spirit, descend upon you and remain with you always. Amen.

5. Final chant

Hymn 'All people that on earth do dwell' (*Praise the Lord*, 138); Psalm 135 (136) 'O give thanks to the Lord' (*Praise the Lord*, 172); Magnificat (*Praise the Lord*, 174).

Service for advent

theme: conversion to Christ

1. Opening part

Entry chant: Psalm 129 (130) 'Out of the depths I cry to you, O Lord' (*Praise the Lord,* 171).

2. Service of the Word

A day or so ago I read the following headings in a newspaper:

> Church robbed
> Road deaths up
> Government deplores attack on member of embassy
> Poisoning suspected
> Attacked man receives no help from passers-by
> Man kills wife
> Not a film for the family
> Police fight with rebels
> Tension between the great powers
> A new type of fighter-bomber

Every day such things are reported in the newspaper. There is always tension, threat, unrest, crime, malice.

Who is, or who are, guilty? We probably do not feel personally guilty for the things reported in newspapers. 'We can't do anything about it', we say, for we are not among the great of this world, and we do not go in for the excesses of gross misdeed.

Who is guilty?

There is much misery that is brought about by reaction to reaction, through more-or-less conscious, voluntary interaction between people. And in those cases where it is possible to point to a guilty person, it is difficult to determine just how personally guilty he or she is. Heredity, upbringing and environment have an extremely deep influence upon a person's behaviour.

It is not much use trying to uncover the degree of freedom in past wrongdoings and of even less use to want to establish who is personally guilty for the failings of mankind, and in what measure.

This much is clear: evil has a power over us, over each of us individually, and over all of us as a whole. It is continually threatening us and we are often no match for it. We suffer from an unavoidable basic sinfulness.

Together we make up this sinful world. We are all guilty. Not one of us is free from blame. We live so close up against and with each other that we can hardly any longer see our guilt and the extent of our harmful influence. We scarcely realise anything of our dependence on others in committing the evil we do commit. Sinfulness is as old as man himself. Each one of us is Adam or Eve. We all desire to have power over good and evil, to make the laws ourselves, for our own honour and glory. We try to be equal to God, to make ourself a god, an egoistic god who knows only himself and the service of himself. We do not make the earth a paradise in which it is good to live.

Each of us could be called Abel, but at the same time Cain. For one does not only kill with the strength of one's fists or of weapons. And he who stands must take care not to fall.

Wherever we live in the world, we human beings are affected by the corruption that Noah already knew. We run the danger of being overcome by a disaster which is of our own making.

Who is not alarmed when he sees these events occuring in the world? What will it all come to? How will our children fare? Will they not be affected or overcome? What guarantee is there that even I will not be affected in a fatal manner by evil elements? Who does not hope for salvation? Who is there who would not wish to be freed from evil? Who does not long for rest?

Evil surrounds us so closely that we can have the feeling of sinking away into a marsh, deeper and deeper, without being able to escape. We should be lost unless a saving hand were held out to us. Also this fear and this longing for salvation are as old as man himself. For they are as old as sinfulness. For this reason the believing Israelite could pray:

Save me, God! The water
    is already up to my neck.
I am sinking in the deepest swamp,
    there is no foothold;
I have stepped into deep water
    and the waves are washing over me.
Worn out with calling, my throat is hoarse,

my eyes are strained, looking for my God . . .
Pull me out of this swamp; let me sink no further,
   let me escape those who hate me,
   Save me from deep water!
Do not let the waves wash over me,
   do not let the deep swallow me
or the Pit close its mouth on me.

[Ps 69: 1–3, 14 f.]

This view of life is gloomy. It is not complete.
God did stretch out his hand. To Noah he gave the
ark, to all generations he gives salvation and liberation. He sends us the ark of salvation. It is the ark
of his covenant with mankind and within it we may
seek refuge and protection; there is room for
everyone. It is the hand of God, lifting us out of the
marsh of sin, whilst the colourful rainbow symbo-
lises the bond between heaven and the threatened
earth.

In the bible we read what God promised to
Noah and his sons and, after them, to the human
beings of all ages.

Reading: Gn 9: 8–17.

Chant between readings: We wish to approach the
God of the covenant with faith and confidence.
Let us sing with the same words and the same
desire for God's presence as the Israelites when
they prayed in their psalm 'Like the deer that yearns
for running streams' (Psalm 41 [42], *Praise the
Lord*, 160).

Reading: At Christmas we celebrate the fact that
Jesus Christ was born. He is the living bond between
God in heaven and humanity on earth. He is the
Son of God, who saves us from the waters of sin

and enables us to love on a new earth. [*Reading of* Lk 4: 16–22.]

3. Reflection on our lives

Brothers and sisters in Christ. The Lord has revealed himself as the bringer of salvation and freedom among men. His work of love has begun amongst us. He does not accomplish it without us, but only with us.

Perhaps we have come here with a heavy conscience, aware of our smallness and sinfulness. Let us test our conscience above all by our attitude towards the Christ.

Do we feel the joys and sorrows of our people and of the whole of humanity?

Are we interested in world events?

Do we experience the needs of others as appealing to us?

Does the threat of sin and evil which is present in the world touch us?

Does this direct our attention to Christ? Do we see in him the One from whom all salvation is to be expected? Do we long for his presence amongst us? Do we give him our attention, so that he influences our lives?

Do we live in hope through him—in optimism?

Do we keep his example of humanity before us?

Do we wish to be aware that Christ calls us to follow his example in working for the wellbeing of humanity and driving off evil?

Do we believe that he can make us into charitable people?

Do we pray to him?

Pause during which music is played.

4. Confession of guilt and prayer for forgiveness

Let us turn to Christ and pray to him to forgive us.

> For having thought too little about who you are,
> Forgive us, Lord.

(*'Forgive us, Lord' repeated by all after each petition*)

> For not having sought liberation by you,
> For having sought our salvation only in terms of our own preferences and interests,
> For not having noticed so much sadness,
> For having so much lacked understanding for others,
> For having evaded our calling as Christians,
> For having been so full of ourselves and our own sorrows,
> For the absence of peace amongst us,
> For racial discrimination, famine and sickness,
> For persecution because of convictions, and for the imprisonment of the innocent,
> For having lived so little with confidence in the future which you will give us,

We pray together that God's kingdom may come amongst us and that the Lord may grant us forgiveness.

All present: Our Father . . .

Reading: Let us listen again to what Jesus says to us: [Mt 25: 31–36.]

Celebrant: All who have sincerely repented, have received forgiveness and grace from God. To all who have asked for new life, for liberation, for strength for a new future, I proclaim God's loving mercy. Christ will be with them, he will preserve them from eternal death and lead them into the majesty of his land. He will protect all his people from being overcome and will gather them into his kingdom.

The blessing of almighty God, of the Father, the Son and Holy Spirit, descend upon you and remain with you always. Amen.

5. Closing hymn

'Praise to the holiest in the height' (*Praise the Lord*, 151); *or*, 'O worship the King' (*Praise the Lord*, 155).

Service for lent

theme: our personal and common guilt

This service consists of a regular alternation between address by the deacon, gospel reading by the priest, and spoken or sung prayer by all present. The most suitable place for the deacon is perhaps the ambo, while the priest might well stand at a lectern in the middle of the sanctuary.

1. *The Organ is played during the entry of the priest and deacon.*

2. *Introductory address by the deacon:* Perhaps this is the first time you have come to a service of penance. Recently much has been said about private confession and services of penance. The situation is rather unclear. Not everyone knows which way to follow. Some people are afraid that services of penance will open the way to an irresponsibly easy ridding of guilt and sin, that private confession will be neglected and will disappear from the minds of Christians. Many are in a state of uncertainty about the actual meaning of the communal celebration, about its significance for the forgiveness of sin. It

153

has become clear that many people are struggling with difficulties as regards private confession, the question as to what sin actually is and what place they must reserve for their own judgement of conscience. Still others ask what they must confess; they do not find words to express their pettiness, their egoism and deep sinfulness. They are stuck fast in old formulas which they have kept from their childhood. Many Christians experience confession as an oppressive burden and as an extra punishment for the sin committed. They do not know what to do with regard to faults which for the moment they still experience as unavoidable. Sometimes they cannot be really sorry for certain things.

What is sin, actually? This is a question that is always being asked. Young people often experience it so differently from their parents, who then ask themselves whether they weren't born too late and who often worry about the threat of a regression in moral judgement.

Through this confusion and uncertainty it has become clear that we all have a need of reorientation in our view of guilt and sin, forgiveness and conscience. This gathering can contribute towards it. Let us give our unprejudiced attention to what is said and arrive at sincere reflection, as we sing and pray. This event should do us good; that is its aim. This is what the Dutch Catholic bishops have said about services of penance:

3. *Priest:* 'These are services in which Christians together express in prayer and song their sinfulness, before one another and before God, in which the priest leads them in reflection upon their life and

calls mercy upon all those who are of good will. . . .
In the gospel Jesus says: 'Where two or three meet
in my name, I shall be there with them' (Mt 18: 20).
The Lord is with us and we may believe that forgiveness of sins is granted to everyone who gives
himself sincerely.' (*Pastoral letter of the Dutch
Hierarchy on penance and forgiveness*, 16 March
1965.)

4. *The Deacon invites prayer in the form of a hymn:*
'Lord, it belongs not to my care' (*Praise the Lord*,
61).

5. *Deacon:* From all that is being said at present
about sin and forgiveness, it often seems evident
that the relationship of man to God is determined or
was determined by fear in not a few cases. Many
lived in a continual fear of committing mortal sin
and asked themselves with great concern whether
they had confessed fully enough the nature and
number of their sins, whether they had fulfilled
their penance accurately, as prescribed. God, for
them, was a stern and all-watchful judge with power
of life and death. When we read through the gospel,
however, we discover that Jesus speaks of God as a
Father who loves us, who knows us, and judges us
from within, whose justice is goodness. For him
there exists no hard, merciless God. Jesus brings
humanity a new faith, a faith in liberation from all
evil, in the forgiveness of all guilt.

6. *Priest:* 'Jesus, on the night before he suffered
death, took bread into his hands, and lifting up his
eyes to you, God, his almighty Father in heaven,
giving thanks to You, he blessed it, broke it and
gave it to his disciples, saying: Take, all of you, and

eat of this, for this is my body. Similarly, when he had eaten, taking the cup into his hands and giving thanks to you, he gave it to his disciples, saying: Take this chalice and drink from it, all of you, for this is the chalice of my blood, the blood of the new and everlasting covenant. It shall be shed for you and for all men for the forgiveness of sins.'

7. *Deacon:* This is essential for man: it is his calling to eat and drink, to live in peace and joy, not to be overcome by evil. For this, man has been created. That is why Christ teaches us to pray to God as the Father of all life, who continues to give life in our daily bread, in the forgiving love of others, in the coming of his kingdom of justice and peace.

Thus praying to our Father means complying with his desires for us, means wanting to live, wanting to belong to his never-ending kingdom.

Let us therefore pray with the words which we have so often used and which may now have a new sense and meaning for us:

8. *All present:* Our Father . . .

9. *Deacon:* All of us here in this church are conscious of our smallness, of our lack of power to love, of our mediocrity. Some—perhaps many of us—are in addition to this aware of having sinned through certain definite deeds and attitudes. These of us will be seeking reparation of their faults and of their peace of conscience. They will thus do well to talk to those whom they have wronged, and they may perhaps feel the need of the deeply personal character of a private confession.

Some of us certainly experience our mediocrity, but do not see what we and we alone should be called to answer for. In this case it is good to ask again here, today, what sinfulness means for each particular individual.

There is in our world much hatred, unfaithfulness, misunderstanding, hardness, dishonesty and lack of respect. 'In our world' means in our country, in our town, in the firm where we work, in our street, in our family. In the sphere of our work we come up against wrongful situations and these we criticise. Do we not forget that we ourselves belong to that work-sphere, that we form elements of that system, that we ourselves help to determine the daily run of events? Perhaps we feel helpless in this regard. We can do almost nothing to change things. But how many people have just as much right to say the same thing? Is no one ultimately responsible, then, or are we all responsible together?

Things happen in our family too. The relationships are not always good. There are days of crisis. We are discontent with this situation, we feel our guilt, and at the same time our insufficiency.

We are friendly with one another, but also realise that we cannot meet each other halfway in everything, that our help and sympathy must remain incomplete. For there is so much that demands our care and our attention; and moreover, we cannot be always prepared for others, not even for our best friends.

Our good intentions sometimes have the wrong effect. Unintentionally we misunderstand one another, we are suspicious, we attach importance to trifling matters. We sometimes let ourselves be led by antipathy at first sight, or just simply do not see another's achievements.

This situation of sinful insufficiency is common to each and every one of us; not one of us can simply withdraw from it. We cannot do other than recognise that it is so; together we shall have to carry the burden of it and at the same time strive towards more harmony and wholeness.

10. *The priest reads aloud* Jn 8: 3–9.

11. *Deacon*: For every failure, for every catastrophe we point to a scapegoat: for the origin of a war, for the horrors that are committed, for the conflicts in our work and the quarrels in our family. We love to point to a guilty person, so that we can then wash our hands in innocence.

Today we want to make no direct accusations against others, perhaps not even against ourself. We want in the first place to acknowledge that we also share in the burden of sin of this world. Therefore let us pray together:

12. *All present:*
I confess to almighty God,
to blessed Mary, ever-virgin,
to blessed Michael the archangel,
to blessed John the Baptist,
to the holy apostles Peter and Paul,
to all the saints,
and to you, father,
that I have sinned exceedingly in thought, word and deed:
through my fault, through my own fault, through my own most grievous fault.

13. *Deacon:* We usually also pray the second half of the Confiteor and call upon the saints in heaven

and the priest in the church to pray to God for the forgiveness of our sins. Today we are not doing this, in order to reflect all the more clearly on what we must do in order to be able to receive forgiveness.

We bear an individual responsibility with regard to the sinfulness of us all, a responsibility that we cannot shift on to anyone else. We are under a duty. Therefore let us listen once more to holy scripture.

14. *The priest reads aloud* Jn 8: 10–11.

15. *Deacon:* This was written so that we should follow Christ's example. It is our calling to show forgiveness to one another and so to make God's immeasurable goodness and mercy visible for our neighbour. Real forgiveness is only possible on the basis of a precise knowledge of ourself, on the basis of the honest reflection that we all do many things in life with a good intention that can cease and become something evil for the other person; only this insight can make us understand the other, make us kind and help us to be forgiving towards our fellow human beings.

Man's situation means that he must often get his hands dirty in order to be able to live responsibly in this imperfect world. Dirty hands—because the production of nuclear weapons is perhaps still unavoidable, because oppression must still be fought against; dirty hands—because independence does not arise without collisions between parents and children, love does not become firm without dissension, and co-operation brings also pain and friction with it.

16. *Priest:* Brothers and sisters, let us cleanse our-

selves by devoting ourselves totally, with all our heart and all our mind, to overcome the evil in ourselves and in the world, so that we may form more and more one united human race in the Spirit of Jesus Christ.

Therefore let us pray:

God, heavenly Father (*All:*) Have mercy upon us.

God the Son, Saviour of the world—Have mercy upon us.

God, O Holy Spirit—Have mercy upon us.

That we may know how to resist the temptations and deceptive appearance of malice, (*All:*) Lord, graciously hear us (*repeated after each petition*).

That we may not succumb to anything that is of evil intent and that threatens us.

That we may take upon ourselves our responsibility for the situation of our world.

That we may keep faith in the victory of goodness and love.

That we may not become discouraged or embittered.

That we may learn to see and accept ourselves as we are.

That we may learn to live with one another's limitations and sinfulness.

That from our hearts we may forgive each other.

That we do not evade our guilt and fall into accusations against our fellow men.

That we may show one another patience and, above all, respect.

That we may experience joy in our relations with each other.

That in all that we do together with others we may have a good judgement of the relative importance of things and a good sense of humour.

17. *Deacon:* Let us now each reflect upon our life for a few moments.
Pause during which music is played

18. To all of you who have come to repentance and who have forgiven your fellow human beings, I proclaim mercy and blessing in the name of God, the Lord of all life.

May God come to your aid with his infinite power, may he forgive your sins and lead you to eternal life. Amen.

May the almighty and merciful God, the Father, Son and Holy Spirit, grant you pardon, absolution and remission of your sins. Amen.

May the passion of our Lord Jesus Christ, the merits of the blessed virgin Mary, and of all the saints, whatever good you do, whatever evil you suffer, bring you forgiveness of your sins and growth in grace, and obtain for you the reward of eternal life. Amen.

Brothers and sisters. Return now to your daily lives. Be humble in your actions on account of your own imperfection; live bravely through your Christian hope; share your food in mutual reconciliation. Bring liberation where there is remorse and concern. Bring reconciliation and patience where there is contrition and grief. Bring new outlook and new life where there is embitterment and weariness of life.

Let us pray:

Lord God, Father, from whom all humanity receives life,

You did not send your Son to condemn the world,
but to save it.
We pray you,
send your Spirit upon us,
that the face of the earth may be renewed,
that all humanity may have life in abundance,
that your peace may be established everywhere.
Then will your name be praised amongst us
and your glory appear in our midst for ever. Amen.

19. *The deacon invites all present to join in the singing of the closing hymn:* 'When I survey the wondrous Cross' (*Praise the Lord*, 68); *or,* 'Praise, my Soul, the King of heaven' (*Praise the Lord*, 152).

Celebration of penance and eucharist

theme: each one of us must be actively on his guard against formalism

1. Opening part

Entry hymn: 'Creator Spirit, by whose aid' (*Praise the Lord*, 86).

Greeting: I welcome you all to this celebration. We usually begin mass by confessing our guilt and asking pardon in the Confiteor. Established customs tend to become mere routine. Often they take place without our giving any attention to them. This is why today we shall try in the service of the Word to direct our attention to the conversion of our sinfulness.

Let us pray for God's mercy: Lord, have mercy. Christ, have mercy. Lord, have mercy (*priest and people alternating in the usual manner*).

Prayer: O God, our Father in heaven; inspired by your Son, Jesus Christ, we have come together here and are trying to unite ourselves in the spirit of his last supper with the apostles.
We shall hear Christ's words, we shall remember his love.

Open our ears and our hearts, teach us to understand.
Then will your Holy Spirit come upon us.
Then we shall be renewed in inspiration and Christian strength.
This we ask of you through the same Jesus Christ, your Son, our Lord. Amen.

2. Service of the Word

When Christ had joined his apostles for supper, these were the words he spoke to them: (*reading of* Jn 13: 33–8)

Pause during which music is played.

During the supper itself, Christ said: (*reading of* Lk 22: 15–20).

Suggestion for the address: We human beings like to be certain about questions touching our existence. Are my sins forgiven? Is God pleased with me? Shall I go to heaven?

Some people are very concerned about this. They eagerly seize upon methods by which they try to assure themselves of salvation. With a fear that is sometimes fierce, they strive to make themselves secure.

To this end they cling fast to the sacraments of penance and the eucharist, to this end they apply themselves to pious practices, from which they expect calm and certainty: they pray exactly three Hail Marys daily, never failing to end the day with an act of contrition.

In reality we do not need to insure ourselves 'against' God. We cannot in any case. Christ gives us certainty, as is evident from the words we have just heard. Of the faithfulness and depth of his love there can be no doubting. He gives his body for us, his blood is poured out for us. With burning desire he wishes to eat the Passover meal with us. Our certainty depends on our answer to his love. 'By this all men will know that you are my disciples, if you have love for one another.' Upon this everything depends. There is no other certainty. The certainty which sacraments, prayers, novenas give us depends ultimately on the question as to whether and how much we love Christ in them and our fellow men in him.

Perhaps we may draw a somewhat rough comparison. It is intended to attract our attention to the danger of routine in our life.

As young children we were enchanted by the fair. Perhaps we were most attracted by a merry-go-round in which we liked best to sit in a little car 'at the wheel'. We proudly raced around at full speed, leaning round bends. Our parents said to us afterwards: 'You really can drive now!', and we were firmly convinced of it. We were so full of it that in the evening we sat at table steering with our plate. Later on, however, we came to a different conclusion. We discovered that we were being propelled rather than moving ourselves, that we ourselves were not determining our direction, but only going round in a closed circle.

May we not compare the little car at the fair with our way of being Catholics?

We have our fixed ways of behaving. We have a whole ritual. We think for ourselves: Aren't we taking the bends fast, aren't we so modern, for we have dialogue mass, the priest faces us, and we talk with self-confidence about everything that concerns the church?

But are we riding on our own steam? Are we really going fast? Or are we just going round and round, without ever leaving our little circle? Do we go forth into the world, do we make efforts sincerely to be united to our fellow men, witnessing with Christian love, with loyalty to duty, and openness to the problems of today? Do we commit ourselves to the people with whom we live? Is their lot also ours, their grief our grief? Do we possess faith that moves us and is leaven in the world? Are we not often just 'routine-Catholics', who think that they have achieved 'being a Catholic' once and for all?

A short while ago someone said: 'The people I work with are all good, careful Catholics. I know for certain that they pray regularly, fulfil their "obligations", and give their children a Catholic education. But at work they are like wolves to one another, they jostle with each other, and begrudge one another success. The most serious part is that they are completely unaware that this cannot be made to agree with being authentic Christians.'

Going to mass on Sunday should, after all, bring us to reconcile ourselves with one another, to share in the one bread, and thereafter do the same in our daily lives.

On Sundays we eat together, but in too much of a routine, streamlined way, too adroitly, and not in a manner that is truly representative of our everyday life with each other. Our life as man and wife, as employee and employer, is taken with us to God's temple too little. We celebrate the mass, but without our innermost existence taking part. We do it perhaps too nicely sometimes, whilst our existence with our fellow human beings is in fact not so 'nice'. When we come here we must try to say 'yes' to one another, to ask and grant forgiveness, to offer one another bread, and promise our support.

The atmosphere of the Last Supper is determined by Christ. He gives out the bread and says that it is his body, given for us. He gave himself. He gives himself, he has bound himself to us.

3. Reflection on our lives

Let us kneel and reflect upon our lives; let this be a meaningful event, not hasty and impersonal, but profound. Let it be a digging down to our basic attitude to life, to what lives in us and occupies our interest.

In this Christ is our example. He gave his body as bread. He allowed it to be broken for our salvation. He precedes us in the attitude of solidarity, of faithfulness through everything, of utter readiness.

Peter thought that he could easily remain faithful to the Lord, whilst he did not yet know what that meant in terms of real life. He did not yet see the task. Perhaps we do not know our own sinfulness because life goes on undisturbed in our little circle and we have never thought about making any effort for the person in need. Do we want to commit ourselves with our whole person to our fellow men and to the community, with readiness to serve, sympathy, solidarity and faithfulness?

Pause during which music is played

4. Confession of guilt and proclamation of forgiveness

Let us say the *Confiteor*

I confess to almighty God,
to blessed Mary, ever-virgin,
to blessed Michael the archangel,
to blessed John the Baptist,
to the holy apostles Peter and Paul,
to all the saints,
and to you, father,
that I have sinned exceedingly, in thought, word and deed,
through my fault, through my own fault, through my own most grievous fault.
Therefore I beseech the blessed Mary, ever-virgin,
blessed Michael the archangel,
blessed John the Baptist,
the holy apostles Peter and Paul,
all the saints,
and you, father,
to pray for me to the Lord our God. Amen.

We ask of you, O God, almighty Father,
give us the grace of conversion and grant us forgiveness,
free us from our sins and lead us together in common unity.

Celebrant: Listen to the words of Jesus Christ, spoken to Peter and reported in Luke's gospel:

Simon, Simon! Satan, you must know, has got his wish to sift you all like wheat; but I have prayed for you, Simon, that your faith may not fail. [Lk 22: 31–2.]

The Lord prayed for us. He will be merciful towards us, forgive us our sins, and lead us into eternal life.

May almighty and merciful God, Father, Son, and Holy Spirit, grant you pardon, absolution, and forgiveness. Amen.

With a small group one might perhaps consider having the people come forward separately after the communal confession of guilt; each person kneels and prays: I acknowledge my sinfulness and I know that I am guilty before my fellow men and before God. *The priest can then in a short formula proclaim mercy and forgiveness upon the person.*

5. Celebration of the eucharist

Seventh service

theme: our relations with others

1. Opening part

Entry hymn: 'O for a heart to praise my God' (*Praise the Lord*, 62).

Introductory Address by the Celebrant: We human beings are continually joining together with others: to work together, to discuss and decide, to hold contests and to practise sport, to watch television, to eat with one another and to provide company, to bear sorrow together and to celebrate happy occasions. We cannot live without other people. This service of penance is a gathering also, precisely because we live together in our everyday lives. Here we shall try to reflect upon our life with each other, in order to find together the true spirit, the Spirit of Jesus Christ, that summons us to form one People, one community of justice, peace and love.

Let us pray for God's loving mercy so that we may succeed in this aim.

Prayer, prayed by all together:

O invisible God, we have come together, although

we hardly know each other, but are all people who are searching:
We are searching for a place in the hearts of others; we are trying to discover how we must live with one another;
we are searching for happiness, understanding and solidarity.
We pray you, approach us in Jesus Christ.
He is the answer given to us by you;
He is your Son, a man with us;
Let his light of love illuminate us,
Let his Spirit come upon us, so that in him we may find each other and with him glorify you, now and for ever more. Amen.

2. Service of the Word

We wish to repent and to obtain forgiveness of our sins. For this we must remember what the Lord asks of us.

> There was a lawyer who, to disconcert Jesus, stood up and said to him, 'Master, what must I do to inherit eternal life?' He said to him, 'What is written in the Law? What do you read there?' He replied, 'You must love the Lord your God with all your heart, with all your soul, with all your strength, and with all your mind, and your neighbour as yourself.' 'You have answered right,' said Jesus: 'do this and life is yours.' [Lk 10: 27–8.]

Jesus summons us to love the people around us. Let us listen to St Paul in order to discover what this summons of Jesus contains:

Reading: Rom 12: 8–21.

Hymn between readings: 'My God, accept my heart this day' (*Praise the Lord*, 89).

Reading: Lk 14: 1–11.

Suggestion for the address: In our relations with each other we are more strongly driven by the pursuit of power than we are perhaps aware. The gospel gives the example of presumptuous self-esteem in taking the first place and ignoring others.

Real love cannot be separated from humility, which is only present when we really 'make room' for and give 'space' to the other person.

Our talk is sometimes a clear attempt to gain power over another person for our own benefit. We try through what we say to get the other into our grasp, by our ready answer, through ridicule, through smooth talk, through attacking an unfortunately expressed statement made by the other person, by bluffing, or by simply not letting the other person get a word in. Holding a conversation demands that we be able to listen, that we give the other person an open space in which to be himself.

We do not recognise or respect him when we twist the meaning of what he has said and straight away conclude in a self-satisfactory way 'You see, I was right'.

We are guilty of violence when we ridicule others, when we give them hurtful names and thereby openly discriminate against them, when we silence them with insulting remarks.

There exist many, sometimes very refined, forms of force for one's own profit. To give a name to some: managing a person at will, to have someone eating out of one's hand, to run a person, to put pressure on someone, and so on. This means that every time we are wishing to 'possess' the other person as an object for our own use. He is to be used as a means to the end which we are pursuing. He becomes an instrument in our hands, he does not receive the chance of being a fellow human being with us. There are always side-motives at play. Someone may be treated by us in a friendly way in order to 'get him where we want him'. We reduce him to an object that we manipulate—we do not approach him for what he is as a human person. In this struggle for power all sorts of means are applied: bribery, attractive promises, abuse of position, false friendship, charm, affected charity or sympathy.

Certain situations easily tempt us into the use of force. The growth of industry and the increase in population demand rigid organisation of the apparatus of government and administration. This offers the possibility of enslaving others by keeping strictly to the letter of the law, the possibility of mangling others in the apparatus of laws, rules and regulations. In a concern where there are many people working, the distance between the lower employees and the management level becomes great. This can encourage the danger of handling the person as a piece of apparatus, the extension of a machine, which at any moment can be replaced by another element.

Every human being forms a mystery, a unique personality with a unique situation of irreplaceable value. In the activity of Christ this is seen clearly. It is characterised by respect for every person, by an attitude of interest, understanding and deep humility.

We all have within us a tendency to lust for power. The child can give a sudden glimpse of this by being cruel to an animal. Youth can be harsh in its collective activities with regard to individuals—to those of its own age, to its teachers and educators—by making life bitter for them and by destructive expression.

Power is seductive. Everywhere: in the state, in industry, in the church, and in the family. As educators we like to drill: commanding is often easier than convincing, ordering easier than discussing. The statement 'I am willing to give anything for my children' sometimes appears an empty phrase as soon as the children take a different path from the one which those who are bringing them up think right or suitable.

Finally, even religion can be pervaded by a search for power. History shows us this all too clearly. And which of us can deny that he also is often searching in his prayer for his own happiness, prosperity and success, but so seldom gratefully approaches God, the Father and Creator of all that lives?

Perhaps we may also think here of the ease and presumption with which we set a stamp on other people. We speak of sinners, unbelievers, schismatics, anticlericals, and so on. We triumphantly judge and condemn, we speak and behave as if we possessed divine power and wisdom.

3. Personal reflection

We shall now pause a few moments in order to let

what we have heard sink in and to obtain insight into our attitudes and behaviour towards other people, towards the neighbours we live with, our colleagues at work, members of our family, and all others whom we judge and with whom we come into contact.

Everything reduces itself to this one question: do we give room to our fellow human being, do we have faith in his desire for goodness and wholesome happiness, do we see a human person in him?

Pause during which music is played

4. Communal confession of guilt and proclamation of forgiveness

Let us pray together:

Lord God, to you, but also to all my fellow men, I confess my guilt in having caused others to suffer under my self-satisfaction, under my selfish disposition, under my love of ease and my desire to rule, to dominate.

From all I ask forgiveness, to all I promise that I will sincerely strive towards greater respect, towards deeper humility.

You, Lord God, I ask to
help me, to help us all,
so that we may truly become your image, your likeness.

Through Jesus Christ, your Son, our Lord, whom we pray to come with the Holy Spirit and dwell in us, today and all days, for evermore. Amen.

Priest: Listen to the words of Jesus Christ:

Be compassionate as your Father is compassionate. Do not judge, and you will not be judged yourselves; do not condemn, and you will not be condemned yourselves; grant pardon, and you will be pardoned. Give, and there will be gifts for you: a full measure, pressed down, shaken together, and running over, will be poured into your lap; because the amount you measure out is the amount you will be given back. [Lk 6: 36–8.]

Because you have sincerely taken part in this service, because you wish to know your imperfection and do better, because you do not wish to condemn but to be compassionate, may the Lord acquit you of all guilt. May he give you a rich measure of well-being, prosperity, and salvation.

May almighty God be merciful towards you, forgive you your sins, and lead you to everlasting life. May the blessing of God, the Father, Son, and Holy Spirit, descend upon you and remain with you always. Amen.

5. Closing hymn

'King of glory, king of peace' (*Praise the Lord*, 145); *or*, 'Now thank we all our God' (*Praise the Lord*, 154).